DIVINE DESTINY
EQUIPPING THE FAMILY FOR
SUCCESS

DIVINE DESTINY

EQUIPPING THE FAMILY FOR

SUCCESS

LINDA CLARK BURLEY

WestBow
PRESS
A DIVISION OF THOMAS NELSON

WestBow Press books may be ordered through booksellers or by contacting:

WestBow Press
A Division of Thomas Nelson
1663 Liberty Drive
Bloomington, IN 47403
www.westbowpress.com
1-(866) 928-1240

Scripture taken from the King James Version of the Bible.

Scripture quotations taken from the Holy Bible, New Living Translation, copyright 1996, 2004. Used by permission of Tyndale House Publishers, Inc., Wheaton, Illinois 60189. All rights reserved.

Scripture taken from the New King James Version. Copyright 1979, 1980, 1982 by Thomas Nelson, inc. Used by permission. All rights reserved.

ISBN: 978-1-4497-7339-7 (e)
ISBN: 978-1-4497-7338-0 (sc)
ISBN: 978-1-4497-7337-3 (hc)

Library of Congress Control Number: 2012920767

Printed in the United States of America

WestBow Press rev. date: 11/12/2012

CONTENTS

PART ONE

RELATIONSHIP

When God placed Adam in a deep sleep and performed major surgery with his rib, Adam woke up and beheld what a gift God had created especially for him. Adam cried from within his inner being and called her woman because Eve was the bomb. She was a brick house. She was bone of his bone and flesh of his flesh. Eve had it going on. According to Adam, it was all good, and God gave them both dominion to rule the world together.

Throughout the years, a microwave generation has taken marriage out of context. Today's generation wants to work its way up the corporate ladder and instantly land CEO positions, but the members of this generation lack basic business management skills. They want to be instant millionaires, yet they have no clue regarding business accounting and money management. As a result of their lack of knowledge, they will find themselves bankrupt or on government assistance. This generation lacks the wisdom of knowing how to build on a solid foundation. "There is a time for everything, and a season for every activity under heaven" (Eccl. 3:1 NIV).

Marriage is so much more than just having sex; marriage requires work. You're working to perfect your relationship and those things you value. Marriage can be a rewarding experience.

It's like working on a puzzle with everything scrambled and out of place. While it doesn't look like the picture on the front cover of the box, as you begin to work with the pieces of the puzzle, you soon discover that the pieces will come together to form a beautiful masterpiece.

Marriage is so similar to that puzzle. In the beginning after the honeymoon stage, after the passion dies and you come back to earth, the real you makes its way to the surface, and all the hidden things you forgot to talk about prior to the wedding seem to emerge suddenly. Both of you have issues. Sadly, neither one of you ever took the time to ask each other about your personal lives.

Now here comes the drama. You're entering into each other's twilight zones, and you're both so different. You're entering into each other's strange, new worlds, but with time, things will fit in place properly. Soon you will begin to see the pieces come together, just like that puzzle. It will fit like a masterpiece. But before your wedding, stop and talk so you won't have any surprises the morning after the honeymoon.

I advise young couples to talk about everything first before making any commitment. Do this during the courting process. Express your concerns and expectations, ask lots and lots of questions, and never feel you are out of place by asking such personal questions. You want to know everything about the person you are planning to spend the rest of your life with.

- What are his or her goals and aspirations for life?
- What is his or her economical and financial status?
- Is he or she knowledgeable regarding money management?
- What is his or her credit and criminal background?

You want to make sure that, after you get married, life for you won't be bankrupt.

You want to know his plans for family planning. You have always dreamed of having a large family, and perhaps he has never dreamt of having children at all. You both need to ask each other these vital questions. You should cover these issues before you both say, "I do."

- Does he or she have a preexisting family from a previous relationship?
- Is he or she single or married?

You would be surprised how many people say they are single when they are actually married with children.

- Does he or she own or rent a home?
- Does he or she still reside at home with her parents?
- Does he or she have his own transportation, or does he or she use public transportation?
- Is he or she employed or pursuing a college degree?

You want to feel secure in knowing that you have financial security for the future. For those women searching for a mate, you should not marry an unemployed man. If he is pursuing his college education, let him complete his degree before committing to marriage. With that in mind, you will know you have financial security for the future because people with degrees are normally hired for better-paying jobs. It is so very important to find out the status of the person you plan to spend the rest of your life with.

Whatever you can think to ask, ask it. Ask about likes and dislikes. Ask about qualities he or she wants in a mate. Now is not the time to be shy. These are vital questions when you search for a mate.

Both of you should be willing to be open and talk about everything concerning your relationship before making such a serious commitment to avoid any issues later. It's good for two people to both have something in common and something to bring to the table.

Seek the Lord in prayer concerning his plans for your life. Ladies, you should not want to marry a man so he can be your bill provider. You should not search for a sugar daddy to take care of you and your babies. You shouldn't be in a rush to get married just because you feel your biological clock is ticking and Aunt Annie thinks life is passing you by. The Lord will always send confirmation of his plans and purpose for your life. So many times, we ignore the warning signals just to fulfill our own lustful desires, and as a result, many people find themselves in wounded and abusive relationships.

SEEK AND YE SHALL FIND

You ask the question, "Where does it all begin?" It all begins with the Word of God."[D]elight thyself also in the Lord and he shall give you the desires of your heart, commit your ways unto the Lord trust in him and he shall bring it to pass" (Ps. 37:4–5). When it comes to the Scriptures, many people have their favorite passages, such as the one listed above that says God will give you the desires of your heart. They overlook the part that says to delight yourselves in the Lord and commit your ways unto him.

"[S]eek ye first the kingdom of God, and all his righteousness and all these things shall be added unto you" (Matt. 6:33). So many times, couples never take the time to first seek God's guidance concerning their lives.

To receive the benefits that God has to offer you, requirements must be met. Think of it like an insurance policy, for example. In most cases, the first requirement is that you must meet your deductible, and after that, you're free to take full advantage of your benefits. Could it be that God just might have whispered something in your ear and you just did not want to hear it? Maybe he is trying to tell you something. The Lord could be telling you to wait. Waiting doesn't always mean no. Sometimes, it just means, "Not yet."

That is one of the reasons why people find themselves caught up in abusive relationships, feeling like they have no way out, like they are living on the ragged edge of life, feeling suicidal, and sometimes committing murder as a means to escape. The decisions you make in life could determine your destiny; they could help or hurt you. Seek the things of God first, and wait for his directions. God will always give you an answer in one form or another. God prepares us for our futures. That is why it is essential to choose the right mate to spend the rest of your life with.

When God gives you a mate, that person will love you with the love of God. I see so many marriages headed for divorce court. Statistics show a high percentage of those marriages concern some Christians couples. You may hear Christian couples say, "God told me this was my mate." In my opinion, this is the perfect reason to justify the things you desire to do. Is God really guiding you to marry this person, or are your fleshly desires getting the best of you? You must be able to distinguish between the two.

For example, you said God told you that this person was your mate. Let's just say you marry this person, and all hell starts to break out. What was God saying when you had to miss church in order to care for the wounds from the fight you had the night before? What was God saying when you put on sunglasses to disguise your black eye? You are hiding and making excuses, but everyone—your church family, your colleagues, and even the members of your community—knows what is going on. What was God saying when you had to drag your mate out of the nightclub as he sat entertaining another woman? Or as you waited for him outside the crack house? Now you are praying for God to deliver you out of all your troubles.

My sisters and brothers, God will not place clean and unclean together because it is impossible for both to walk together. You are listening to your heart instead of your mind. Your heart is the state of consciousness having to do with the arousal of feeling and excitement. It all revolves around what you are feeling. On the other hand, the mind is our state of reasoning, the thought of reality. Your mind pays attention to the things around you. The mind perceives and observes, and it heeds. The mind takes care of and watches over you.

Your heart is saying, "I'm so in love with this person, and love will cover a multitude of sins." But deep down inside, you know this person has issues dealing with jealously. He may have already told you that he has problems with other men looking at you. Your mind is saying, "Caution! Caution! Red light! Red light! This person has issues!"

Your mind is also saying, "Here we go again, another rollercoaster of issues. Caution! He will break your heart. Caution! Red light! Red light!"

It's a matter of wrestling with self and selfishness. Self is a factor of adjustment meaning you now have to regulate and conform and go through the changes in order to keep up with him, and in the midst of trying to keep up, you began to lose your own identity. All the signs are right in front of you.Family and friends may warn you that this is not the right person for you, but you choose to follow your heart, thinking it's God's will for your life.

Sisters and brothers, God will never place you in an unhealthy situation. God wants the best for you because he loves you just that way. It will be up to you to make the right decisions for your life. Be prayerful and seek the things of God so you will not fall for the snares that Satan has to offer you. It is a dangerous thing to end up sleeping with the devil.

SEARCHING AND SINGLE

Never allow anyone to rush you into making quick decisions. Remember, this is your life. You must learn to make wise choices because the decisions you make could cost you for the rest of your life. People who enter into marriage for the wrong reasons, nine times out of ten, are headed for disaster.

Do not use marriage as an excuse to fill the voids in your life. Some issues will take God to deliver you out of. It is unfair to have someone step into your life who is unaware of the types of luggage you are carrying. You must deal with your demons first before inviting anyone to share your life. You must be able to identify who you are and find yourself. God has destined the directions of your life. He has made you a new creation, and he came so you might have life. In him, there is liberty. You can do anything through Christ that strengthens you. You're more than a conqueror through Christ Jesus.

You first start with identifying who you are. God can deliver you from all your past issues. You will never be able to go forward until you put your past behind you. Know within yourself who you are. At times, no one will be there to affirm you and tell you how lovely you look.You don't need anyone to tell you. Know within yourself who you are. You are a gift to creation. When you begin to realize your worth, you can take a look in the mirror, snap your fingers, and call your own self "blessed" because you will realize you are God's finest creation at that moment.

To all my sisters out there suffering from low self-esteem due to a broken heart, sister girl, you are bold and beautiful. Everything about you is unique because you're an original and worth waiting for. Don't sell yourself short for any man, and don't be so desperate that you settle for just anything. You will be in for a rude awakening because that person will break your heart one day, especially when you thought you were the only one in his life.

Let's just say you meet a man who you thought was everything you ever dreamed of having. He may whisper sweet things in your ear. He may tell you everything you want to hear.He promises to give you the world. He may tell you how much he loves you and touch you in the right places, sending chills up your spine, but you have only been acquainted with this person for a few short months. You know nothing concerning his background, but you feel you have met your Mr. Right.

You have let your guard down, and you have completely opened yourself up to this person—your mind, body, and soul. You think the next step will be wedding bells.You have already begun to imagine what the day will be like. You wait by the phone, hoping he will call you. When you call him, he's too busy to talk, or you get his voice mail, saying to leave a message and he will get back with you, but he never returns your calls. His visits become fewer and fewer.

Now you're left wondering what is really going on. Then finally one day, he just happens to answer your call and basically informs you that the relationship is over and he has found another lover. In fact, he goes further to say that the other woman is much more compatible than you are and she meets his every need.

By this time, you're wondering whether to strangle him or bust a cap in his behind. You need all the prayers you can get just to keep your composure. You are not in the spirit to pray. All you think about now is revenge and how you can get back at him. He has hurt, humiliated, and disgraced you. You introduced him to your family and friends. He even came with you to church one Sunday. What are you going to do now, and what will people think? You gave this person all you could give, and that was all of you.

Could it be, baby girl, that you set up your own self for a fall? He had all of you—your mind, body, and soul—before he ever made a commitment to you. You were committed to him, but he, on the other hand, did not share the same sentiment. If you are good enough to sleep with, then you're good enough to make it legal first. If he cannot commit to that, he is not worth your time. You are a rose. A rose is just a rose, beautiful and full of blossom, a gem cut in the image of God. You are costly, baby girl. You're one of a kind.

Marriage is a mandate by God. So many couples choose to play house before marriage. If things don't work out, the marriage is out the window, and they go their separate ways because there is no level of commitment. Ladies, never place yourself in a compromising situation. If he loves you, he will be willing to wait forever or however long it takes because you are worth the wait. During the process of courting, you're getting to know each other, and that takes time. Don't allow anyone to rush you into a relationship just because he wanted to get you between the sheets. You might just be in for a rude awakening.

WHAT'S LOVE GOT TO DO WITH IT

Tina Turner had a song in the eighties; "What's Love Got to Do with It?" a song that could have came straight from Tina's heart. Tina married Ike Turner, a man who didn't value her as a person with so much to give. Ike only valued what Tina could do for him, which meant Tina's talent was a profit for Ike Turner. The marriage ended in divorce as a result of abuse. Life for Tina was hard, and Ike was Tina's meal ticket to a better life. She was talented. She could sing and dance. Ike basically rode on Tina's dress tails. Tina lived a life filled with unhappiness, abuse, depression, and suicide attempts. It was a life filled with hell, and after being beat so many times, she decided that enough was enough.

"Everything that glitters is not always gold." I bet, if Tina had to do it all over again, she would have done things differently. Coming through the storms of her relationship with Ike made Tina stronger. She was able to let go of the pain from the past and create songs that empowered women going through similar situations. She helped them realize that they too could take a stand and be strong enough to walk away from the pain of an abusive relationship. Sometimes you must let go of the hurtful things in your life in order to fulfill God's given purpose.

Don't sell yourself short for what God has for you. It's worth waiting for. God wants to give you the hidden treasures of this world. Don't go treasure hunting without a compass to guide you, or else you might get lost. God is your compass, and he's the only one who can lead you to your hidden treasures. You don't want to find yourself in a relationship where you have to fight your way out of it, as in the case of Tina Turner. The basics to living a happy, healthy life are based on love.

Anytime you love someone, you do not want to see him or her hurt. In marriage, you're committed to each other. You are partners, and you should have each other's back. I hear men and women always say, "There are no good women and men out there anymore."

But they do exist. God will never run short of a few good men and women. 1 Kings 19:9–18 tells the story of a prophet who gets very discouraged because he feels there was no justice. People were not keeping the laws of God, and many prophets had been murdered under the hand of Queen Jezebel. Elijah felt he was the only prophet left keeping the laws of God, but God had news for him. God directed him to get up from his pity party because he had a job for him to do. God had chosen kings to be over Israel. Elijah's instructions were to go and ordain these men, and then God encouraged Elijah with the news that he had seven thousand people in Israel who had not bowed down to Baal.

So don't think all the good people are distinct. God has not chosen to reveal them yet. Do the right things, and wait for the promises God has for you. Don't sell yourself short for anyone. You're God's precious gift, and you're worth the wait. If you're a virgin, be proud of what you stand for. You are a precious vessel. It should not matter what others may say or think.You are highly esteemed and favored in God's eyes.

Why is it so important to stay a virgin until marriage? It is a covenant of love ordained by God, reserved for the season you share with your mate. Baby girls, you are special. Don't buy the garbage that guys pitch to you. It's an old deception when they say, "Prove your love for me, and let's have sex."It should be the first signal to run and not look back. Your body is precious, a vessel unto God, and you don't won't to share it with just anyone or everybody.

I realize we are living in a New Age generation. Most young ladies will not agree with me, and you can love me or hate me, but I'm just being real and telling you the truth. Why does God insist that young women stay virgins until marriage? Let's see what God has to say about this subject. Deuteronomy 22:13–21 states,

If a man takes a wife and, after sleeping with her, dislikes her and slanders her and gives her a bad name, saying, "I married this woman, but when I approached her, I did not find proof of her virginity," then the young woman's father and mother shall bring to the town elders at the gate proof that she was a virgin. Her father will say to the elders, "I gave my daughter in marriage to this man, but he dislikes her. Now he has slandered her and said, 'I did not find your daughter to be a virgin.' But here is the proof of my daughter's virginity." Then her parents shall display the cloth before the elders of the town, and the elders shall take the man and punish him. They shall fine him a hundred shekels of silver and give them to the young woman's father, because this man has given an Israelite virgin a bad name. She shall continue to be his wife; he must not divorce her as long as he lives. If, however, the charge is true and no proof of the young woman's virginity can be found, she shall be brought to the door of her father's house and there the men of her town shall stone her to death. She has done an outrageous thing in Israel by being promiscuous while still in her father's house. You must purge the evil from among you.

This law was meant to enforce premarital sexual purity and to encourage parents to instill the values of sexual purity within their children. It's hard for young people to listen to the parents' instructions when parents are doing the very same things. You tell your children what not to do. You tell them not to smoke because it's bad for their health, but you smoke. You tell them not to drink alcohol, but alcohol fills your cabinets. You tell them not to hang out in clubs when they know where to find you on Saturday nights. You tell them not to engage in sex, but they see you coming home with different men, closing the bedroom doors behind you.

You are a parent living a double standard. If you expect your children to respect the rules you lay before them, then you, in return, must live by example.

Normally, an engagement lasted for twelve months, and when the young man came to ask the girl's parents for her hand in marriage, he had to have some credentials. He had to have acquired something in life that was of worth. This young man had to prove to the young woman's parents that he could take care of their daughter when he took her to be his wife. He also had to bring gifts that were of worth to the young woman's parents. A box of candy was insufficient. He couldn't come empty-handed with just anything because he would most assuredly leave without a promise. The young woman's parents would not consider the young man a good candidate for their daughter.

So many times, couples rush into marriage, and the young man had not attained anything in life. He has limited resources, education, and finances. They have no prior planning for the future and no parental blessing. They marry for love, but they have not counted up the cost. Love can't pay the bills and put food on the table. When there is a lack in finances, couples begin to have marital problems, which results in divorce in most cases. In my opinion, it is not up to the woman to take care of a man. If the man wants to make her his wife, he should be financially stable before taking on such a major responsibility.

In the old Testament during the courting process, the couples were never left alone for one second. Her family was always present during the duration of the engagement. Physical contact—including hugging and kissing—was forbidden. These can jump-start emotions to running.

Mama used to say, "If you can't stand the heat, get out of the kitchen." and "Where there is smoke, there is fire." Mama knew what she was talking about. Christians in the dating stage need to be careful during this time. If a young man wants to come over to your place and have Bible study, the Bible won't be the only thing he will want to study once he gets there.

Ladies, keep a level of integrity for yourself. You're too good to be spoken evil of. If the young man has respect for you, he will not suggest your place or his for the evening. He will see you to the door and keep on trucking.

New Age men and women are more aggressive nowadays. They want to try it out first to see if they like it, and if they get straight to the point, they only look for a booty call. Mama used to say, "Why buy the milk when you can have the cow for free?"

Why would he want to marry you when he can have his cake and eat it, too? You're only fooling yourself. A man will respect a woman when she respects herself first.

In the bible if the man brought an accusation against the young woman, her parents were obligated to produce proof of her virginity, as with the bloodstains on the bed sheets. The evidence was a bloodstained garment or a bed sheet from the wedding night. Once a man breaks the seal of her virginity (the hymen, a thin mucous membrane or passage lining that covers the opening of the vagina) and enters her chambers, a spot of blood is produced that gives proof she is a virgin. If the blood was not produced, it meant she was not a virgin. Anything that has never been opened requires some type of pressure in order to allow access.

Can you imagine your parents sitting outside your door, waiting for you to consummate the marriage so they can take your bed sheets to the elders of city to determine if you are a virgin or not? Records from various cultures in ancient Middle Eastern countries refer to this kind of evidence being made public. If the parents offered such evidence of her virginity before the marriage, then the man who made the false charges was to be whipped and had to pay the parents more money than he first paid for the young woman. It would be double the original bride price because he too was slandering. That is, the accusation questioned the young woman's father's desire or ability to pass on values regarding sexual purity to his children. Also, his daughter was given a bad name. Support for the wife and perhaps the legal right of her firstborn child was protected by the forfeiting of the man's right to ever divorce his wife.

On the other hand, if the husband's charges could not be disproved, then the wife was to be stoned at the door of her father's house. Not only was this harsh punishment intended for the sin of fornication or being promiscuous, it was also for lying to her prospective husband and presumably implicating her father in the deception.

This evil was to be purged from the nation. Virgins were young women who had not engaged in sexual intercourse with a man. This term was sometimes used to describe the nation of Israel to emphasize its purity and holiness as the chosen people of God.

Some of you are saying, "I've been there and done that. What's next?" Thank God for his love, kindness, and mercy for sending his son Jesus Christ to allow humanity another chance at life. "Christ has redeemed us from the curse of the law, being made a curse for us for it is written cursed is everyone that hang on a tree. That the blessings of Abraham might come on the Gentiles through Jesus Christ, that we might receive the promise of the spirit through faith" (Gal. 3:13–14).

If we lived under the old law as it was written, that would wash out more than half the women of today because the penalty for sex outside the marriage was death. There was no hope except through the cross and shedding of blood by Jesus Christ. So if you have been there and done that, you can't turn back the hands of time, but now you have a better understanding of the importance of keeping yourself pure before marriage. Start from where you are. Perhaps you are single and searching. Realize your worth, and wait on God. He has a purpose in mind for you. You might not have been aware of the importance of keeping yourself holy. God does hold us responsible for the things we do not have knowledge of, but when the truth comes, we are then held accountable for our actions. Keep yourself holy unto God. He will divinely send you the right mate in due season.

It's important to wait on the Lord. When a woman has sexual intercourse with a man, she actually takes on the spirit of that man and becomes one with him. You don't want to hook yourself up with someone who is not fully hooked up to God.

Did you not know that you take on the spirits of each person you have had sexual contact with? Every time you see that person, your heart will pound, and you will long for them. He will be on your mind even though the relationship is over. He will have gone on with his life, and you still will be holding on to the past. That person's spirit is a part of yours. You can't go on without him, but he has gone on without you. It will take the hand of God to deliver you from all the spirits you have entangled yourself with so you can leave the past behind and get on with your life. Be careful who you hook yourself up with.

PREPARATIONS PRIOR TO SAYING "I DO"

You want to be married, but are you prepared to take on such a big responsibility? In every stage in life, there is preparation. When we entered elementary school for the first time, we were not qualified to graduate the following year. There was a process of preparation—from elementary school to junior high and then high school, a total of twelve years to complete.

Following high school, we are required to enter another level of higher learning, college. When you go out on the job market, you're required to attend a job training program first. Education and employment are the essentials to life planning, and if training is required, then wouldn't you agree that, along with everything else, there should be preparation before marriage? So many young people are unprepared to care of themselves, let alone a spouse and children.

Have you ever come across some women who don't know how to do anything but look like a supermodel? The girl may have it all going on. She works an eight-to-five, Monday-through-Friday schedule. She spends all of her money on buying clothes. Whatever she wears looks good. Her hair and nails are always up to par. She looks like a runway model. She always has it going on ... until you step into her apartment. She has beanbags for furniture. Her home looks as if you stepped right out of the seventies era. Her dining room consists of patio furniture. Her bedroom furniture is what she accumulated when she left home. Her hospitality is unspeakable. She may offer you lunch that consists of a ham or cheese sandwich served on a paper plate, complete with a disposable cup of tea with no ice.

Honey, do not even ask to use her powder room because it has been known that sister girl forgets to buy toilet paper. Just hope for the day you drop by for a visit that she has a roll on hand, or else you will be stuck in a bad situation. Sister girl definitely doesn't have it going on in the homemaking department.

Young men out there also run their lives very much the same way. He looks the part but does not have his priorities in the right place. He rents an apartment but doesn't have furniture because he spends all his money on clothes and cars. Or perhaps he still lives under his mother's roof at the age of thirty.

These two types of people are the perfect example of poor performance. They're both in for a fall before the roller coaster begins. They invest more in themselves rather than their future. They're two peas in a pod who live for today and not for the future.

You have to learn how to balance both worlds. Live for today but also plan for the future. If you start planning early, your future will look bright. Most young people do not have a savings account. They're not educated on how to balance a checkbook, and if they have the privilege to get a credit card, they abuse it by charging up everything they can get on credit. They are not knowledgeable concerning their credit score. Three things will follow you all the days of your life: your birth date, Social Security number, and credit score.

By the time they reach thirty, many young people already face financial problems. They want to live for the now instead of investing in the future. When you find yourself in debt, you're in a system that dictates what you can and cannot have. You place yourself in a situation that, instead of being a homeowner, you have to rent because your credit isn't good enough to buy a home unless God intervenes on your behalf.

But young people start their families early without prior education and job skills. They start to have children at a young age without planning, and it's hard to attain good-paying jobs without a good education. As a result, they are caught up in the system where they have very little choices. Considering their situation, they either are forced to get a job with low wages and no benefits or rely on government assistance.

With government assistance, you are caught in a catch-22 because now you are stuck in the system that dictates the type of jobs that you work. For example, if you earn too much income, you're ineligible for government assistance, so they want you to earn just enough money to depend on the system. This cripples you, and you're stuck in a system that never advances your future.

Many parents have no other choice but to work and go back to school in order to attain a better income for the family and future. If you plan early, you will continue to plan your life for the future. You won't have to worry about depending on government assistance. Prior planning prevents poor performance, so start planning now for your future.

Looks are just temporary. You may look like you have it all going on, but looks can be deceiving. Good looks won't put food on the table. If you cannot do the essential things required to have a successful marriage, you will have problems within six months. I often hear single women say,

> When I get married, I'm not going to be stuck in a kitchen all day, and I am not cleaning up behind my man because he's grown and can do it himself. I am not going to have to cook because we will eat out for dinner most of the time. I'm going to get a man who loves me whether I cook or not.

What do you think my response was to that? "Girls, are you crazy?" Hello! Wake up, and smell the coffee. This is not a soap opera. Honey, this is the real world. Get real. You have been looking at too many reality shows. No man will marry a woman who can't cook, and you have to have a good-paying job in order to eat out every night. Girlfriend, you better take a cooking class and buy a few cookbooks because you will be single for a long time.

It is essential to learn how to cook and clean up after yourself before bringing someone else into your life. Young men need to learn to be proficient in cooking and cleaning as well. There is no excuse for a young woman nowadays to say she cannot cook. Several cooking shows are on television today. You can get cookbooks and recipes online. There is just no excuse. I have never seen so many male chefs. In my day, we really didn't have any choices on learning how to cook. We only had a few cooking shows, the most popular being Julia Child. We didn't have Internet, and we had to learn by process. If you know how to cook and clean up after yourself, nine times out of ten, you're on your way to planning your future. You are learning how to be a good mate.

Being independent is an essential. James Brown has a song that says, "I don't need anybody to give me nothing. Open up the door. I'll get it myself." Don't wait to get married for a man to give you something. Learn independence, and get it yourself. Learn how to cook, clean, work, and buy your own stuff. Have something to bring to the table so that, when you meet your mate, you will have something to give back as well.

It is so sad when I see women looking for a man just so they can get married to get a house, car, and money. Why not be independent? Get up, and get it yourself! Never enter into a relationship of marriage expecting someone to pay your bills. Take responsibility for yourself, and learn how to be independent and pay your own bills.

Ninety-nine percent of marriages end in divorce mainly due to financial setbacks. The pressures from being bogged down with bills can cause stress for many families. There can be a number of reasons for having financial setbacks, for example, a death of a spouse, loss of employment, and lack of financial planning, to name a few.

Before entering into marriage, I strongly suggest attending a financial management course. It better prepares you for the future, and in the event that a setback should occur, knowing how to get through the tough times will better prepare you. Nothing in life prepares us for loss, but just knowing what to do in times of crisis can be a benefit. Prepare for your future. Don't just spend money unwisely just because you have it to spend.

Learn to save for your future so that, when the time comes and you're ready to settle down and have a family, you will enjoy your life and have financial security. Prepare now so you will be ready when God sends you the gift.

HOMEMAKING 101

When I was in school, one of the requirements for graduation was taking home economics. Homemaking taught you the basics to being a good homemaker. It was the science and art of home management, including household budgeting, knowing how to be a wise shopper when it comes to shopping for food, clothes, and childcare, and eating the rights foods for a healthy diet. These courses prepared young women and men for adulthood.

Being a homemaker was definitely not on my agenda. Homemaking was a pastime for me, and plus, it was the easiest course to get a passing grade in. I had many dreams, one of which was to become a singer. I could always sing. I grew up singing since the age of four, and I grew up in the church and always sang in the choir.

I also dreamed of becoming a fashion model. I had the looks and the right weight. I had also taken a course in modeling. I had dreams of living in a mansion and driving a different car each day. I dreamed of going to Hollywood and being discovered in the spotlights. Oh, yes, I had dreams for myself, and being a wife with a house full of babies was not one of them on my agenda.

After attending a sewing class for a semester, I found out that I had a gift for sewing. I had even thought about going to school in Paris one day and being a fashion designer. I was going to be a cosmopolitan woman.I did not want to be bound to traditional habits. I wanted to be my own woman doing many things in the business world.

Annie (Madea) and Walter Clark were my distant aunt and uncle who adopted me when I was two years old, I had other siblings but they were adopted by different family members. In some African American families, it was normal to address the matriarch as "Madea," short for "mother dear." It is a term of endearment and respect.

I had a wonderful childhood growing up. Mama and Daddy Clark saw to it that I lacked nothing. I was always dressed in the prettiest of dresses with lace socks and shoes to match. I was their only child, and they treated me like a little princess. I never recalled ever having a hungry day. I had so many clothes, and Mama had to store my winter clothes to make room for my summer ones. When my ex-husband and I first got married, he said he had never seen anyone with so many clothes.

I had a well-rounded childhood. Daddy worked for a truck driving company; Mama was a homemaker. She worked part time ironing clothes for the white folks, the Gilcrease. They were really nice people. They knew Mama had a small child at home so they arranged to bring their laundry to our home. When Daddy was not working, he was at home with Mama and me. We had a large family.

Family and friends always filled our home, especially during the holidays. My mother was a great cook and homemaker. Before she met Daddy, Mama was the head cook for a local diner called Tuckers, where the military soldiers often patronized for dinner on the weekends. They, along with her family and friends, loved Mama's cooking.

Mama always kept our home nice and clean. She liked the finer things, and she would buy things that looked expensive at bargain prices. Mama believed you should always look your best wherever you go. I am grateful she instilled those same values in me, which I implanted into my children.

As a child growing up, I would always have the pleasure of watching Mama cook in the kitchen. She brought out the best aromas with the different spices she used. Daddy didn't have to eat out. He had the best cook in our kitchen. Even with watching Mama cook, being a homemaker was just not what I wanted to do, so I ignored the basics to what Mama was trying to teach me. She even bought me a Betty Crocker cookbook, but I only enjoyed the desserts.

When I was sixteen, a group of my girlfriends and me decided to get together and bake a cake. We didn't have a clue on how to bake a cake from scratch, but I had written down a recipe, and all we had to do was follow simple directions. My friend Karen and her sister Sonya read the directions, and I added the ingredients. We were going to make our first official pound cake.

My friends and I had no clue of what we were about to embark our lives upon. It was easy, and anyone could do it ... or so we thought. We mixed all the ingredients together just as the recipe called for. Sonya, Karen's sister, greased the pan, and I poured the batter in the pan and placed the cake pans in a 350-degree oven, just as the recipe instructed. We were so proud of ourselves, in spite of the disaster we created in the kitchen. Flour was all over the counters and floors. Eggshells were scattered from one end of the table to the other. While the cake baked, we cleaned the kitchen. The whole room looked like a science project gone bad. We cleaned up so Karen's mom wouldn't have a heart attack the moment she walked in from work.

When our cake was ready to come out of oven, it smelled so good. We were so proud, but when we pulled the cake from the oven, it was a different story. It had dropped below its normal size. We wondered what went wrong. We had added all the ingredients the recipe called for, so Karen went over the recipe instructions again. Four cups of flour, yes ... three cups of sugar, yes ... one teaspoon salt, yes ... eight eggs, no.

"My mother only adds four," responded Karen.

Okay, four sticks of butter, yes ... two teaspoons vanilla extract, yes ... one teaspoon of baking powder.

"Oops, I forgot to add the baking powder," said Sonya.

Now we knew why the cake had come out looking like a stone. Karen's brother thought it was so funny. He grabbed our cake and ran like someone was chasing him out the door. He and his friends made such a joke of our disaster that they proceeded to play touch football with our pound cake, as we were standing there silently in humiliation. We watched our cake go flying through the air. It never even broke a crumb. I vowed that very day that I would never attempt to bake a cake again. I would leave all the cooking up to Mama.

Prior to meeting my husband, Daddy Clark passed from a heart attack six months before I turned fifteen years old. Daddy had three cardinal rules:

1. I had to graduate from high school.
2. I had to attend Prairie View College.
3. I had to acquire a professional trade, like a nurse, teacher, or secretary.

Back then, black folks didn't have many choices. To be a black woman and an attorney was unheard of. Daddy always said he did not want his daughter to have to struggle the way he did when he was young man. Daddy was strong-minded when it came to education. He felt I had opportunity he didn't have growing up. Dating and marriage was not even in the picture according to Daddy's wishes.

Mama didn't feel as strong as Daddy did when it came to education. She gave me more space. She allowed me to start dating with her supervision, and she insisted that, in order for me to go out on a date, one of my cousins had to chaperone. When Daddy died, I felt that Mama wanted to get on with her life. Leaving a young girl home alone without parental supervision was not good because it created a window for promiscuous behavior.

Please, darling hearts, never allow your mother to lie for you and say you did all the cooking when your mother actually prepared all those great dishes. One Saturday evening, I invited my future husband over for fish dinner. I knew fish was one of his favorite foods. The way to a man's heart is food, and I wanted his heart, so I knew Mama was just the person to get me there. I told Mama to prepare a fish dinner and say I did it. She prepared a great meal, which kept my soon-to-be husband's appetite coming back for more. Mama must have lied her head off because she was trying to get me hitched off. My mama got us through the evening. I played my props, and everything turned out perfect. My future husband was so amazed about my cooking skills that we were married six months later.

The truth would finally come out that I did not know how to cook, iron, or wash clothes. I had no housekeeping skills at all. I had to learn the hard way, and my husband probably would have loved to strangle my mother for lying. Suddenly, reality would soon set in, and I would be introduced to the real world. Much to my surprise, I would actually regret not paying attention to my homemaking instructor and Mama.

Their teachings would have really come in handy for later years to come.

Six months after my husband and I got married, we soon discovered we were about to have a bundle of joy. I couldn't cook and almost starved my husband to death. We ate a lot of fast food. Fried chicken was my best friend. We ate chicken for breakfast, lunch, and dinner, and when we were not eating chicken, we were hanging out at the hamburger stand.

At times, we would drop by my mother's house for a bite to eat. I will never forget the day after our wedding. My sister and I got together and decided we would surprise my husband with a pizza. It was a disaster. She or I didn't know anything about making a homemade pizza. We threw some dough together, thinking off the top of our heads. We decided to make a vegetarian pizza. We added everything to that pizza, including canned corn, string beans, and even spaghetti sauce. Then to top it off, we added cheddar cheese. We placed it in the oven and waited for the timer to go off. We waited for my husband to get home from work to surprise him. He took one look at his dinner and suggested takeout at the chicken stand, of course.

I was not prepared to be a young wife or a mother. I was only seventeen years old. I could not wash. Whites and colored clothes had only one thing in common. They were all dirty, and they all went into the washer at the same time. As a result, white blouses turned out pink or had multiple colors. After twelve months of marriage, our clothes had dwindled down to nothing. If I didn't change the colors of our clothes after washing, I would shrink them in the dryer.

By then, the Burley family was growing. I had one baby on the way and another one hanging on to my dress tail. After the first year, my husband was so drained from starving and looking homeless. Somehow I had a strong notion he felt like shipping me back home to my mother with no return address.

Darling heart, you must find a man who loves you for better or for worse. I strongly advise young women to prepare themselves before you get a husband so you know you will be able to take good care of him. If he is not in it for the long run, he will be out the door in a heartbeat.

In another incident, I wanted to do something special and surprise my husband when he got home from work. So I washed his robe along with other white and colored clothing as usual. I mixed the clothes together and washed them in hot water. I then transferred the clothes from the washer to the dryer and set the dial on extra hot. And when the drying process was complete, I removed the clothes from the dryer. They were all faded as usual.

I searched around for my husband's robe but could not find it. I separated the children's clothes from our clothes. I couldn't find his robe anywhere, so I looked in the washer. No robe. I looked in the dryer. Still no robe. I was baffled as to where the robe could have been. I thought perhaps I had just overlooked it and forgot to put it in the dirty clothes basket or left it in the car by accident. I searched the car all over and still did not find any robe. I decided to search through the children's clothing once more, and I couldn't believe my eyes. From the time the robe entered the washer to the time it went into the dryer, there it was, hidden in the children's stack of clothing. I didn't recognize it because it had shrunk from a man's medium size to a tiny tot's size. Oh my God!

I felt like I had just committed a cardinal sin. How could I have messed up so badly? This robe was very sentimental to my husband. He had never been without this robe since the age of eight. He was crowned king in this robe at his church pageant as a little boy. On his shoulders laid this royal blue velvet robe that draped the floor as he walked and upon his head a crown to be king for a day. This robe became one of his childhood cherished memories. His mother took care of this robe until I got a hold of it. I held the robe up in front of me just to make sure my eyes were not playing tricks on me.

Oh my God! I thought to myself.

To my disgust, I was definitely looking at the right robe. So I folded the little robe and placed it underneath all the children's clothes in the basket. I raced home so I could arrive before he did, all the while trying to figure what story I was going to come up with. In the meantime, I hid the robe among the children's clothes and prayed to God he would have a memory loss concerning his royal blue robe.

Months had passed, and I had totally forgotten about the robe until my husband asked me one day, "Linda, have you seen my robe? I was going through some of my clothes and noticed my royal blue robe was missing."

I said, "What royal blue robe?"

He said, "You know, my favorite royal blue robe I was crowned king in when I was just a little boy."

I asked, "Which one was that? I don't recall. Perhaps you misplaced it when we were moving."

He replied, alarmingly, "I don't have that many clothes left to store."

I realized I was not going to get around this story so I shamefully went and got the robe, held it up where he could take a good look at how I had ruined it, and held my breath.

He looked like he had seen a ghost. "What in the hell is that?"

I said, "Your robe!"

He said, "Whose robe?"

I said, "Your robe."

He said, "No, not my favorite robe. Not the robe I was crowned king in. Not the robe my mother took care of for years. Not my freaking robe."

He dropped his head with a shake, took a deep breath, and walked silently out of the room without saying another word.

"But honey," I responded with tears in my eyes, sobbing like a child.

I felt like such a failure. I felt as if I couldn't do anything right. Finally, after a week, we kissed and made up. But from that day forward, he was determined to care for his own clothing, what little he had left to savage.

After Daddy died, Mama decided she would get back in the dating stage again. She met an old friend named Duncan and fell head over heels for him. She didn't have time to teach me the basics of being a good housekeeper again, and I desperately needed a touch from an angel. God had an angel standing in the wings to teach me homemaking 101, Bernice Chandler Scruggs, my mother-in-law. She was a God-fearing woman who prayed continually. She was a saint. She had the gift to look into your life and tell you what God was doing. She knew your past and your future, and she was always on target. God revealed things to her in dreams and visions. She saw things in me I didn't see in myself. She would always say things like, "And one day, God will use you."

I was young and wanted to enjoy my life. I was not ready to be converted, but she never pushed her religion on me. God had given her wisdom on how to handle a young girl like me. She handled me with lots of love and care. She knew I was a handful.

If she had been like most mothers-in-law, she would have clawed right into me, trying to figure me out. I would not have been a good candidate to share her son's life.

While she carried my husband in her womb, she had already declared what he would be. Mother Scruggs was converted shortly after my husband was born. He was to be a preacher, straight from the womb of his mother.

I had no preparation on being a wife and a preacher's wife at that. I thought to myself, *What in the world have I gotten myself into now?* I was the type of young girl who didn't want anyone to tell me what to do, especially when it came down to correcting me. I hated being corrected because I felt I knew it all. How foolish of me when, in fact, I didn't know anything at all.

For a short period, we stayed with my mother-in-law. I thought I would just suffocate and die. Mother Scruggs was the Martha Stewart of her time. She did it all: the wash, cooking, and cleaning. And, oh, did she clean. An inspector could take a white glove and wouldn't find a spot of dirt on the glove.

One day, I was doing our laundry, minding my own business, when Mother Scruggs cleared her voice and said, "Linda, would you mind if I just showed you something?"

"Sure," I said.

What now? I thought.

She said with a soft voice, "Honey, it's important when it comes to the care of your clothes that you wash them properly."

I said nothing but stood there shaking my head in agreement with a crack of a smile. It's important to separate your clothes, your white with the whites and your colors with your colored. That way, your white clothes will be real pretty, and your colored clothes are not faded. Not only did she tell me how to wash properly, she showed me how to measure my detergents properly. Normally, I would just pour washing powder into the machine. I wouldn't measure it, and I would just pour bleach right in the water on the clothes. You get the picture of what a mess it was.

Mother Scruggs continued to instruct me. You have to wash colored clothes in cold water and your whites in hot water. I pretended I was taking it all in, but the moment she left the room, I thought to myself, *She's not my mama. She can't tell me what to do.*

I proceeded to place all the whites and colored clothes together, pour the detergent on the clothes without measuring, add the bleach, and set the dialer on hot. Then just as I went to turn, Mother Scruggs passed by the kitchen. The washer was located between the kitchen and dining room. She glanced right at me, but she never said a word. She went directly to her recliner in the living room, pulled out her black Bible, and proceeded to read her daily devotional.

I felt like an ass because, once again, the clothes came out of the dryer faded and shrunk, looking funky. Mother Scruggs never looked up. She just continued reading. The one person who took the time to teach me something I didn't know. And I needed all the help I could get. I wouldn't even allow her to help me. I was so foolish, but I didn't realize that, from that day forward, Mother Scruggs began to plant seeds into my life. I wanted to prove to her that I could pay attention and not be a Miss Know-it-all.

A week after she showed me the correct way to wash, I decided to try it the way she had taught me. I separated the whites from the colored clothes. I set the correct temperature, hot for the white and cold for the colored. I measured the detergent just as she had showed me. I pulled up a chair and waited for the cycle to complete, and when the washing was complete, I placed the clothes in the dryer.

So far, so good, I thought to myself.

When the dryer was complete, I pulled out the clothes. Lo and behold, they came out looking nice. I was dancing in the kitchen with so much excitement. I had finally done something right with the help of a great mother-in-law.

I ran to her bedroom door and knocked on the door. She was praying, but I did not care.

She slowly opened the door. "Linda, is everything all right?"

"Look at the clothes I washed. They didn't come out stained or shrunk and looking funky."

With a smile on her face, she looked through the clothes. "I knew you could do it."

I felt as if I had won an Academy Award. Now that I was learning how to wash, I had two other major problems. I could not iron or cook. I was dangerous with an iron. My husband's good shirts ended up with designs from the iron, not the manufacturer. He always had the designs of an iron on the front and back of his shirts. I ruined so many of his good shirts. Sometimes I would just tell him I lost them on the way from the Laundromat. In truth, I couldn't bear to tell him I had just ruined another one of his good shirts. I was really trying hard to be a good wife and mother. I was doing my best, but to my husband, my best was not good enough. His mother taught him to iron, and he taught me the same.

Whenever we would go over to Mother Scruggs's house, she was always ironing for her husband, Reverend Scruggs, a pastor at the local church. She always made sure his shirts and handkerchief were washed and starched. She would say a preacher had to always look his best. I would pay attention to the way she would iron clothes. My husband ironed his clothes for a while until he could trust me with an iron again.

With time, I did learn how to iron. After so many years, my husband got fed up and bought me a cookbook. It was one of the best gifts he could have given to me. From that cookbook, I began to learn how to cook and measure ingredients properly. To this day, I still have that old cookbook.

I was blessed so many years ago to have a supportive husband who was willing to stick around to see what the end would be. But not every man would be willing to stick around waiting for you to learn the basics of good housekeeping, so make sure you learn the essentials before saying "I do." If I had stopped long enough to listen and learn the basics, I would have been prepared to be a good homemaker, but I had to learn the hard way.

Darling hearts, learn all there is to learn before you settle down and have children. Perhaps you have no plans of settling down, but you should still learn how to cook, iron, and clean. Those are the essentials to taking good care of you. If you can't take good care of yourself, how in the world will you be able to take care of a mate and children in the future?

I wanted to share some of my experiences with you because I realize the importance of prior planning. Sharing your life with another individual can be a wonderful time in your life, but in order to make it work successfully, it starts with the fundamentals. You have to lay the foundation and ask God to prepare you for your mate. Wait on God to send you what you need, and once you have received what God has for you, learn to nurture and care for it. God will never give you anything you're not prepared to handle. Marriage is a ministry of divine love.

Learn to appreciate each other's individualities and God-given abilities. Identify the laws of reconciliation and forgiveness.

When God made man, it was all good. God said it was not good that man should be alone, so God created him a helpmate. They were no longer two but became one flesh, and it was all good in the eyes of the Lord. "So they are no longer two, but one. Therefore what God has joined together, let man not separate" (Matt. 19:6 NIV). That word will stand from here to eternity.

God has ordained the marriage relationship to be in order. He has ordained that man be the head of the home, and the head of every man is God. A woman can follow a man anywhere when she feels secure in knowing he has directions, dreams, aspirations, and potential. He just won't settle for anything that life has to offer him. If this man follows God, which is a bonus, then a woman can follow him to the ends of the earth because she knows God directs his steps. She can follow a man who follows God.

PART TWO

BUILDING ON A
SOLID FOUNDATION

Express yourself so there won't be any surprises that could destroy what might have been. You will occasionally have disagreements, but sit down and talk it all out, your feelings and frustrations. Be willing to lay everything on the line, and be honest about what you're feeling. Be careful and consider each other's feelings. Be willing to make changes in your relationship.

Ladies, let your mate know how you feel concerning certain issues. Gentlemen, be open to communicate your frustrations with your mate. Don't keep anger and frustration bottled up inside. It will only lead to further problems down the line. Just exhale and release. Ladies, if there is a problem in your relationship, open up and communicate your feelings. When he asks you what's wrong, don't reply by saying nothing when you know what you're feeling. Maybe it was something he did or didn't say. Perhaps it was just the wrong timing, or a number of things could have made you frustrated.

Is it that time of the month? Ladies, we all know our hormones tend to get unbalanced and out of whack. Our mood swings can get out of control. At times, it's like we have two personalities in one body. We tend to be this way during the most inopportune time. At times, you just don't want to be bothered or touched.

Cramps can be so unbearable. Sometimes you may wonder what God was thinking when he created the menstrual cycle. Some men cannot fully comprehend what a women experiences during her menstrual cycle. It would be so nice if God allowed man to have a menstrual cycle for only one day. They would just die. I could just see it now. They wouldn't be able to handle it, but they would understand how important it is to give a woman her space during this time.

Not all men can fully understand. My sisters, it's your job to break it down and explain how you feel. Don't have a brother confused. Explain to him that you experience mood swings and head and body aches during your cycle. It has been said that a women passes about a 2-3 tablespoons of blood during her menstrual cycle, which leaves a woman feeling drained and exhausted of strength and emotions. For the brothers who wonder if it was something he said, just be sensitive to her feelings, and remember that life will be back to normal within a few days.

Many years ago, my menstrual cycle was never pleasant. It seemed like I cramped for twenty-four hours a day for the whole week, yet I was responsible for caring for the family. At times, I didn't feel like getting up to cook, wash, clean, and run errands. I felt like my husband didn't have a clue of what I was going through. One day, I decided to show him. I called him into the bathroom and let it all hang out, the blood, the clots, and all. I insisted that he sit there and look at what I was about to reveal to him. I gave him the basics of how a woman feels walking around all day with a wet pad on, a house full of screaming children, and a husband who didn't understand. He was totally shocked.

I was definitely not having a very good day, and I just wanted to express my feeling. And what better way to do it? I felt no shame. He was my husband. From that day forward, his perspective was totally changed. He told me later that he had no idea what a woman really goes through during that time of month. He said every man should have the experience of seeing a woman give birth. It makes a man honor and respect the mother of his children. But if a man actually sees what a woman goes through during her menstrual cycle, he will understand and respect her more and give her the space she needs.

Whatever the reasons for your frustration, sit down and talk it out. Lack of communication is one of the reasons why so many marriages end in divorce. It can become a cycle of silent misery just waiting to explode. Many people bottle up their frustrations for years, refusing to talk about what is really bothering them. They repress their anger, that is, hold back and restrain so strictly or severely as to prevent the natural development of the expression of their feelings. Marriage is an investment whatever you deposit into it. That's just what you will receive out of it. Similar to the banking process, in order to gain interest, you must make regular deposits. A deposit is something entrusted for safekeeping, earning interest, a rate of increase that is paid when the money is in use. Savings is a long-term investment that will pay off with time. To invest into a bank or company is to obtain profit.

Marriage is similar to banking investments. Whatever you take the time to invest, with time, you will be able to take advantage of the benefits with interest.

Marriage is more than just having sex. It is a lasting friendship between two adults, sharing deep and tender feelings for one another. Disrespecting your mate in front of others or even comparing him or her to others will never help the situation. It will only make matters worse. Express your likes and dislikes.

You can both sit down and jot down a list of the things you like about your mate, along with the things you dislike. Perhaps you love all the attention he gives you, but you hate when he hangs his underwear on the back of the door or does not raise the toilet seat up, leaving sprinkles on the toilet seat. You may love how he buys you flowers when it's not even your birthday or anniversary, but you hate when he's lost and doesn't pull over and ask for directions. You love her cooking, but you can't stand her nagging. You love how clean she keeps the house, but you hate when she stays on the phone for hours at a time with her girlfriend. You love the way she dresses and smells when she goes out, but when it's bedtime, you hate to see her with a head full of rollers and that ugly robe she has worn for years.

You enhance one another. You are supposed to bring out the best in each other. Marriage is devoting yourselves to each other, sharing passion, your hopes, and your dreams. Marriage is a close intimate union between two people coming to a common ground, helping each other to develop, being mindful of each other, and being careful not to criticize one another when you're around others. In marriage, you will have disagreements, but know how to disagree.

Never make statements in the midst of an argument you may regret later. In the heat of the moment, you may say some things you don't mean and make irrational decisions. Anger can bring out the worst in people. Stop and think about the consequences before you say something that can come back and bite you later. My mother used to say, "Don't let your mouth get you in trouble."

Compliment and bring out the best in each other. Marriage is all about enhancing one another. If you are experiencing a financial situation, don't tell your mother that your man never has any money, it's been so long since the last time he bought you a dress, and you almost forgot what a new dress looks like. Perhaps he tells his mother that you're so backwards that you don't even know what forward looks like or you can't seem to get anything right. When you do these kinds of things, you only tear down a reflection of yourself. You're talking about your mate here. If you're not satisfied with your significant other, then make changes for the positive.

What can you do to change the atmosphere? If you know your mate is a good person and you both have loved one toward another, perhaps a financial loss has brought you to this point. Sit down and think of ways to solve the problem. Pray for your mate, and build each other up. Share your dreams, hopes, and aspirations. I advise you to be discreet with people you share your personal business with. At times, you will need to confide in a friend or family member, so be careful who you allow to come into your space. You can't share your problems with certain individuals because they are nosy and don't intend to encourage you. They just want to know your business so they can spread the word of what's going on up in your house.

In a marriage, sometimes you will get angry and say things you don't mean, causing you to sleep inches apart in your bed, or you may not talk to each other for days, but that does not mean you do not love one another. It goes back to sitting down and talking it all out. Know when to sit down and talk. Timing means everything.

One of the major keys to having a successful relationship is to be honest with one another. Marriage is not easy. I'm not telling you it's going to be easy. Whatever is important to you, you will take the time and invest into it. Marriage is a long-term investment for better or for worse ... 'til death do you part.

Marriage is an investment of love, faithfulness, commitment, respect, and foundations to build upon. It will work if you work it.

Faithfulness means being reliable and loyal. In other words, when you stood in the presence of God, you stood in solemn oath, committing to a binding pledge that you would be loyal to the person you chose to spend the rest of your life with 'til death do you part.

Many people take their vows lightly. They just want to say they're married. They don't understand they are sharing their dreams and disappointments and being there in the good and bad times and in times of sickness and even death. You are a friend, lover, and partner. You meet each other's needs unconditionally. This is what true love is all about. It's more than just making wedding preparations, making sure everyone shows up for the big day, setting the stage for the evening, walking down the aisle to meet your knight in shining armor, sharing that special moment together, and sliding in between the sheets for a night of ecstasy.

Here's a question! After the wedding guests are gone, all the excitement dies down, and weeks, months, and years pass by, how would you define your relationship then? Were you in it for the thrill? What were your reasons for saying "I do"? Did you realize your biological clock was ticking and you still had no man with everyone asking when you were going to get married?

A marriage should have three important ingredients: faithfulness, honesty, and love. If these three are not included, you will be in for disappointments. Your fantasy world will tumble down around you. If you entered into the relationship for the wrong reasons, let's talk about honesty for a moment. Honesty means to be creditable and respectable. You don't lie or cheat. You are trustworthy. One of the formulas to having a successful marriage is honesty. This honesty should have been in order prior to saying "I do." It is all a part of the getting-to-know-you stages. You are letting it all hang out, revealing the real you.

You should not wait until the day after the wedding to find out you just slept with Dr. Jekyll and Mr. Hyde, only to figure out later that you have just stepped into a den of unresolved issues. Talk it all out. Be open-minded when it comes to communication. Learn to talk and to listen, being sensitive to the needs of each other. Just being a good listener can be the antidote to solving many problems. Sometimes people just want you to listen and not try to fix the problem. Sometimes they just want you to understand what their needs are. Sometimes husbands can be unsympathetic toward their wives' feelings, most likely because they have never really been taught how to nurture.

For example, boys are usually first given toy trucks, tools, and cars. As a child, they are taught to fix things. They fix their truck and car. They will hammer on this and that. They watch and help Dad fix the automobile. They take toy things apart to see how it is made, only to rebuild it back up again. They are taught that the man guards and protects, like Tarzan. Tarzan is always swinging through the trees, trying to rescue Jane out of a problem. In fact, Tarzan was always trying to solve everybody's problems.

On the other hand, a little girl's mind is wired to nurture. She is given dolls. She loves and cares for her dolls. She washes and combs the doll's hair, and she dresses the dolls and rocks them to sleep. She will gently pet the dolls for comfort. She has been programmed to play the mommy role. She will imitate her mother because this little girl will one day grow up, get married, and have a family of her own to care for so she will be better prepared with time. Our mothers did not prepare us to be business executives. We were trained to be good homemakers, whereas the little boys were taught to fix things.

Most young men are not taught the basics to being a good husband and father. In our society, 75 percent of the homes is absent of a father figure. No one is there to teach them how to be a husband and father, and many of these young men have to learn by experience. Many young men have a drive to be a better father than what their father was, and many young men learn to be good husbands and fathers from role models and leaders within their community.

To nurture means to give tender care to something. Some men feel that, if their mate is having a problem, she needs to figure it out, fix it, and get over it. A woman sometimes just wants to know her man is concerned about her needs, and it helps to take out time to give her a big hug and kiss, letting her know how much you care and not expecting anything like sex in return. Give the lady what she needs. Let her know how much you love and appreciate her and you will be there to see her through whatever she is enduring. Communication is the answer.

Some people don't stay committed to their vows simply because they were not steadfast in the first place. That's why some people choose not to get married. Instead, they choose to live together to see how things would work out. Darling hearts, never allow a man to just want to live with you first to see how things will work. Honey, he can walk out of your life just as fast as he came in with no kind of commitment, and you will have no legal rights over your assets depending on what state you reside in.

Some men will defend the common law marriages by saying vows are just words written on paper. I disagree with your view because you're standing in the presence of God, making a promise before God. You're making a covenant, a contract to one another, just as God committed he will be our God and we shall be his people. God has married his people. This relationship can't be annulled. Common law has no binding vow or commitment. You're not married according to the laws of God.

There is order when it comes to the things of God, and if we want to please God, we have to do it his way. In order to be in the plan of God, we have to be obedient concerning his Word. There is a story in the Bible of the woman at the well in John 4:3–29.Despite her lifestyle, this woman had four husbands, and the man she was sleeping with was not her husband. Jesus let her know that she had to change her way of thinking and line up with the order of God. He told her , everything she ever did, Jesus was there to meet her need. He had the answers for her remedy, and he changed her world. He challenged her to make the difference.

No one ever took out the time to tell this woman why it was wrong to sleep with one man after another, but Jesus did and made the difference in her life. Are you sleeping with someone who's not committed to you?

I used to pray that my marriage would be just like my in-laws, a match made in heaven. They were both faithful to one another. The years went by. My mother-in-law became very ill, going back and forth to the hospitals. She was constantly having one stroke after the other. My father-in-law never left her side. Finally, when she could no longer care for herself, the decision was made to commit her into a nursing home. I know it must have been a very difficult decision for my father-in-law because he always wanted to care for his wife, but he was limited because of his own physical conditions. He was also sick at times.

Dad Scruggs never abandoned the woman he fell in love with. My father-in-law had a full-time job caring for a sick wife. At the same time, he was responsible for pastoring a church full time. He was at the nursing home, morning, noon, and night. He tried to assist the nursing staff by helping them to rotate Mother Scruggs back and forth. He would try to feed her and do the things he could do to make sure she was as comfortable as possible. Even when she was so very sick and things looked dim, he would glance over at her and sweetly tell her how beautiful she was. He would lean over the bed and give her a gentle kiss, caressing her forehead as he whispered sweet words into her ear. Sometimes I would catch their eyes connecting with each other's. She could not communicate, but just having him there made the difference. They were inseparable.

Being there in the good and bad times, that's faithfulness. I really tried to pattern my own marriage after my in-laws. Their relationship was a marriage of love divine. It's good for your children to see you being affectionate with each other, just for them to see you laugh and talk together and hug and kiss one another.

When I was young, my parents were always around. I truly believed they loved one another, but I never saw them being affectionate with one another. Men are taught to never show emotions. I never saw my parents hug and kiss. I never saw them share tender feelings toward one another. My parents were strong-minded people. At times, they would argue and disagree, mainly due to me. I was a daddy's girl, but Daddy was strict in some areas. If it were something I really wanted to do and I knew Daddy would not allow it, I would side with my mother because I knew she would allow me to do it when Daddy went off to work, which would result in their arguments. When Daddy found out, he was very upset until my mother figured out what I was up to.

My parents communicated well with each other. When Daddy got paid, he brought his checks home. They sat down at the table and figured out their bills. I would have loved to see Daddy chasing Mother around the house, seeing them laugh, hug, and kiss each other. But because I never saw this kind of interaction between them, when I saw how my in-laws treated one another in their relationship, it was strange to me but nice to see. After staying with my mother-in-law for a short period of time when my husband and I first got married, I began to see what real love and marriage was all about. They did not allow their children to get in between their relationship, that is, one child siding with the other parent to get his or her way. They had pet names for each other. She would call him Honey or Daddy; he would call her Mama or Honey.

They were happy together, and they did everything together. He was a local pastor as well as a cook. They even owned a couple restaurants. They loved cooking together, preparing delightful dishes. Dad Scruggs is known for making the best coconut cream pies. Whenever he preached, Mother Scruggs was right on the front seat, cheering him on.

She made sure his shirts and handkerchiefs were white, neatly starched, and ironed. Whenever Dad Scruggs left the house, he didn't have a wrinkle on him. He always looked his best. At times, she didn't quite agree with him on certain issues, but she never discussed anything in front of neither her children nor the church laity. If she had anything to say, it was always done in the privacy of their bedroom.

She was an elegant woman and full of wisdom. As I stated earlier, when we were first married, we stayed with Mother Scruggs for a short period of time. I had not heard any argument, fussing, or fighting. They only spoke to each other with the highest respect. I was not used to this kind of formal behavior. It was strange for me. I was determined this was all an act and I was going to get to the bottom of it. I felt married people were not this close to each other. Their bedroom was next to ours, and when they would retire for the night, I would put my ear to the wall and see if I could hear any kind of fussing. Much to my surprise, I heard just the opposite. I would hear them talking peacefully to each other, sometimes praying or sharing a Bible discussion together. Once in a while, I would hear giggles and wonder what that was all about. I could only imagine. For the short period of time we stayed with them, I never heard them arguing with each other. I would call my mother over the phone and say, "Mama, these people have one strange relationship. They don't argue, fuss, or fight."

I would later discover why this marriage was a match made in heaven. Dad Scruggs was a pastor of one of the local churches, and Mother Scruggs was a licensed missionary. Both were out of the Church of God in Christ, a deeply religious movement that practiced exactly what the Bible teaches. My parents, on the other hand, were not deeply rooted in religion. My mother was raised Baptist, and Daddy only attended church to help Mama deliver her dinners for the church on Saturdays. Our church was right across the street, Greater Grandview Baptist Church. We attended services three times out of the week.

Now compare this to the Pentecostal services my in-laws attended. They had services six days out of the week, not including revivals and district meetings. However, my parents loved to party with family and friends. I was accustomed to someone cussing someone else out, which at times was not taken seriously. The typical African American family could party on Saturday, but Sunday was the Sabbath.

Mother Scruggs, on the other hand, did not party. She was deeply committed to the church. She was one of the sweetest ladies you would want to meet. She would not hurt a flea, but on the other hand, my mama didn't take any mess from anybody. She always carried her twenty-two-caliber pistol in her purse. She carried that pistol everywhere, including church, and slept with it under her mattress and a Bible on her nightstand.

Mama took the preacher literally. When the Bible said, "Watch, fight, and pray, "Mama kept her piece at all times. Mama's best friend was named Annie. They looked just like sisters, and they always had protection on them. I would always hear the stories of when they were young and how they had razors strapped to their nylon stockings. They would not hesitate to use it if they had to. In their time, they were some bad divas, and they did not take any mess off anybody, not even their own husbands. They always had each other's back. They were around during the heat of segregation. They were strong black women of their time.

Mama passed a few years back, but Aunt Annie is now ninety years old, in her right mind, and as beautiful and sassy as ever. These are the kind of people I grew up around and loved so dearly, so now you can understand how I came from two different classes of people who had different beliefs and behaviors, one class of people who didn't believe in nonviolence and another who believed in turning the other cheek. One believed in protecting yourself by any means necessary; the other believed in praying for your enemies.

I was always told the story of how Mother Scruggs, before she was born-again, was a razor-swirling diva as well and could handle it anywhere at any time. Dad Scruggs always said Mother Scruggs had the heart of an angel and she was the best thing that could have ever happened to him. He used to tell us the story of when he was so very ill that the doctors didn't expect for him to live. He had to go to a hospital located in another city. They had specialists there who could treat his illness. He would tell us how Mother Scruggs would get on the Greyhound bus to travel back and forth to see about him. She would spoon-feed him like a baby when he couldn't feed himself. She never left his side during his recovery period. Their finances were affected because he was unable to work due to his illness. He said there were many days when the family went without, but she never complained.

She made do with what she had. Dad Scruggs was ill for about six months. She had to take care of a husband and children, and for that, he never forgot. People always say that Mother Scruggs had gotten to a point in her illness that she no longer recognized anyone anymore, but I always disagree. Before she lost her eyesight, she recognized Dad Scruggs when he walked in the door. She recognized his deep baritone voice as he greeted the nurses down the hall. She knew when he was there and when he was absent. The moment he stepped in the room, a peace came over her, and nothing else mattered.

Dad Scruggs sat in her room until the wee hours of the night, and as soon as she slipped off to sleep, he quietly glided away. This is a love story of what marriage is supposed to be about, being faithful and being there in the good and bad times, when things seem to be falling apart, and when it sometimes feels like life is not fair. For better or for worse 'til death do you part. Will you be there:

- In all his physical attractiveness?
- When beauty turns to frailness?
- When illness and disease take a toll on the physical body?
- In all his masculinity and physical power?
- When his health begins to deteriorate and determination begins to weaken?
- To wipe the tears from his eyes?
- To feed and clothe him when he can't do it himself?
- To clean the many messes he will make?
- To pray for him when he can't do it himself?
- When your voice is the last one he hopes to hear?
- Holding his hand as he leaves this world and sets sail to eternity?
- Kissing his forehead as he quietly slips away, realizing your eyes will be the last one he will see?

This is what being faithful is all about. These are some of the keys to laying the foundation of a good marriage being there for each other.

LOVE AND RESPECT

I was speaking earlier about how couples are supposed to treat each other. Everything in marriage should be centered around cultivating and taking special care of one another's needs. Marriage is similar to gardening. There is a process to good gardening.

We lived in Germany for a period of time. My two German friends, Elizabeth and Omar, gave me the keys to good gardening. For one, you have to turn the soil over, that is, rotating. You have to remove all the hard minerals that have formed in the soil over the years and all the unwanted plants that have grown wild in places they're not wanted. If you don't take this step, it will destroy the growth process.

You must provide certain substances to aid the plant growth process, that is, fertilizing. It is spread onto the soil to increase the ability to support plants during the growth period. In one process, the German farmers used manure over their soil. It consisted of animal excrement often mixed with straw, and they used it as a fertilizer.

We stayed in a small village. Right across the field was a large farm that grew all sorts of vegetables. For the first couple months, the whole village smelled of manure. Imagine waking up to the smell of dung. Not only did the larger farmers implement manure into their soil, the local people who grew plants and the people with backyard gardens also implemented manure into their gardens. The smell was very unpleasant, which only lasted for a few weeks.

Once the soil had been treated and fertilized properly, next would be the planting process. Seeds are planted on an area of land, and then the land is irrigated to provide water for the crops. Water is needed for the plants to grow healthy. Within weeks of planting, seeds begin to grow into new individual plants.

In the nurturing process, this involves watering and making sure your plants get plenty of nourishment and sunshine. During this process, you're giving tender care and protection to your young plants, just as if they were your children, helping them to grow and develop. You keep out the insects that can destroy a young plant. Pretty soon, you will begin to see an outgrowth on a stem or branch, consisting of a shortened stem and immature leaves or flowers that eventually turn into beautiful mature flowers or vegetables. Soon it will be time to gather the ripened crops or just watch how beautiful the flower has blossomed. Now you can gather a basket of beautiful flowers to beautify your home with the sweet scents from the labor of your hard work.

During the summer seasons, I would love to sit back in my chair and gaze at the different plants I had planted. In one section was my vegetable garden. I could smell the scents from the cucumbers and strawberries. The mustard greens looked so lovely. The okra had grown so tall. In another section, I could smell the beauty of the flowers with the blend of different colors. My backyard was so pleasing to look at, to touch, to smell, and to taste. I would often catch my neighbors looking over my fence to admire the beauty of my garden. It required a lot of groundwork giving them all my attention, making sure they were properly taken care of.

Similar to gardening, you must cultivate your relationship. You have to discard the things that will slow down the process of development, such as the rocks, the weeds of those past relationships, unresolved issues, and things that should not come between the cores of your relationship. It is a sin to throw up your ex-lover during the heat of an argument. You will have disagreements at times. Just don't allow the sun to go down on your anger. Don't say things like, "If I had married Bill, my life would have been so different … If I had married Lilly, she would have made my life easier … I should have never married you."

Anger can cause you to speak out of hurt from your feelings. When the anger boils down, you will be grateful you did not speak what you wanted to say. Learn to fight fair. Keep your past relationships out of your intense arguments. These weeds should be removed from the root and destroyed because it will filter in and destroy your fruit.

Cultivate your relationship. Spend time with the one you love. Share in his or her interests as well. Everything should not be centered on your needs only. Devote time, and create enjoyable activities that will enhance the relationship, which brings about strength and desirable qualities to each other.

THE UNBELIEVING SPOUSE

You must be wise when it comes to dealing with a spouse who is an unbeliever. For example, what if he or she were a believer when you first met and got married? And for whatever reasons, he or she is not as devout as he or she once was. What do you do? Do you continue with the relationship, or do you count your losses and get out of the relationship? What's at stake? What do you do?

Ask God for wisdom and direction in such a delicate matter. It's not always a good idea to listen to everyone's advice, but the leading of God will work wonders in a relationship. God can perform miracles. He will leave you in awe and amazement.

So many times, we try to fix things ourselves, and in the midst of trying to help out God, we only make things worse. God will answer you concerning your relationship. Sometimes we can get so impatient and annoyed at the waiting process. We are so eager to fix things on our own, and we don't wait long enough for God to do things. Many couples, especially Christian ones, are so eager to run to divorce court, trying to get them out of a chaotic situation. Many find themselves in the position they are in simply because they did not inquire God's answer when they first entered into the relationship. They just dived in "heart first" without thinking about the consequences later.

So when the relationship turns sour, they start praying and give God an ultimatum, "Lord, if you don't fix this thing, I will fix it myself." Ultimatums do not move God. He moves in his own time, and it's up to you to follow by faith.

I stand very strong when it comes down to spousal abuse. I do not believe that a spouse, whether male or female, should continue to live under such an environment. Abuse, whether physical, psychological, or sexual mistreatment, is harmful, improper, and illegal. It could cost you your life and the lives of your children. A man is not a man when he can beat and verbally abuse his wife. You can't beat anyone into submission. You're only enslaving him or her, and it makes the person being abused despise you even the more. I believe that, if a person finds himself or herself in such a cruel environment, he or she should look out for his or her own safety, along with the safety of his or her children.

In some situations, divorce is not always the answer, but separation for duration can cause some people to think about their actions. Time will cause some people to look at themselves in the mirror and consider how they treat others. Time has a way of healing. There are other cases where the best results for the sake of the family are to divorce because some people will never change. The family becomes unstable and unhealthy, which will create problems down the line for the children. Some relationships weren't worth getting together in the first place. God knew it, and now your eyes have become open to the things that were closed.

Ask God for guidance in the crossroads of your life in those critical and troubled times. It's important whose voice you hear when you're in the valley of decisions. Be careful of the advice you entertain because you may not know that God is working behind the scenes to fix things on your behalf. That's why it is essential to pray and ask God for his directions. When you're searching for an answer, everyone is there to give his or her opinion.

"Girlfriend ,if I were you ..."

But there is a difference. They are not you, and they can cause you to make a decision you otherwise would not have made so quickly. Go to God, and seek his Word concerning your situation. God sometimes speaks to us through dreams, visions, people, and the Bible. Pray and hear the Word of God concerning your situation. Don't be so quick to run to divorce court without a word from the Lord.

MARRIAGE AND DIVORCE

Should Christians divorce? What did Jesus say about divorce?"It has been said, 'Anyone who divorces his wife must give her a certificate of divorce.' But I tell you that anyone who divorces his wife, except for sexual immorality, makes her the victim of adultery, and anyone who marries a divorced woman commits adultery"(Matt. 5:31–32 NIV).

> "If a man marries a woman who becomes displeasing to him because he finds something indecent about her, and he writes her a certificate of divorce, gives it to her and sends her from his house, and if after she leaves his house she becomes the wife of another man, and her second husband dislikes her and writes her a certificate of divorce, gives it to her and sends her from his house, or if he dies, then her first husband, who divorced her, is not allowed to marry her again

after she has been defiled. That would be detestable in the eyes of the Lord. Do not bring sin upon the land the Lord your God is giving you as an inheritance" (Deut 24:1–4 NIV).

Some Pharisees came to him to test him [Jesus]. They asked, "Is it lawful for a man to divorce his wife for any and every reason?" "Haven't you read," he replied, "that at the beginning the Creator 'made them male and female,' and said, 'For this reason a man will leave his father and mother and be united to his wife, and the two will become one flesh'? So they are no longer two, but one flesh. Therefore what God has joined together, let no one separate.'"Why then," they asked, "did Moses command that a man give his wife a certificate of divorce and send her away?"Jesus replied, "Moses permitted you to divorce your wives because your hearts were hard. But it was not this way from the beginning. I tell you that anyone who divorces his wife, except for sexual immorality, and marries another woman commits adultery" (Matt. 19:3–9 NIV).

Everything that God does, he does in decentness and order. When he ordained marriage, it was established both in heaven and on earth. He implemented certain stipulations that were clearly understood. A man or woman could not divorce for any reasons. As Jesus responded to the Pharisees' questionings, you had to have grounds for divorce. Let's see what the apostle Paul's views were when it came down to the question of divorce.

Let's look at 1 Corinthians 7:10–16 (NIV).

To the married I give this command (not I, but the
Lord): A wife must not separate from her husband.
But if she does, she must remain unmarried or else be
reconciled to her husband. And a husband must not
divorce his wife. To the rest I say this (I, not the Lord):
If any brother has a wife who is not a believer and she
is willing to live with him, he must not divorce her.
And if a woman has a husband who is not a believer
and he is willing to live with her, she must not divorce
him. For the unbelieving husband has been sanctified
through his wife, and the unbelieving wife has been
sanctified through her believing husband. Otherwise
your children would be unclean, but as it is, they are
holy. But if the unbeliever leaves, let it be so. The brother
or the sister is not bound in such circumstances; God
has called us to live in peace. How do you know, wife,
whether you will save your husband? Or, how do you
know, husband, whether you will save your wife?

In some situations, as I explained earlier, many spouses find
themselves caught up in abusive relationships, and sometimes
the only answer is a period of separation or divorce for the
well-being of that person. In the society we live in, people are
divorcing every week for any reason to get out of the relationship.
Irreconcilable differences are the main cause for divorce. So
many couples use the excuse, "We're not compatible ... My mate
is impossible to live with ... We have nothing in common."

These were some of the vital signs to watch out for during the
dating process. People don't change overnight, and just because
you get married, that does not mean you have the power to change
that person. Whatever is hidden on the inside will eventually be

uncovered. Were you so in such a hurry to get married that you just ignored all the signs that were right in front of you? People divorce these days because they conclude that marriage is not for them and they prefer the single life.

Marriage is a union of two people coming together, committing to one another, and intending to live together as partners. You can't live the single life and be married at the same time. The two will clash somewhere down the line. If you want to party with your single friends all night long and then come home to a mate who is waiting up for you, that will only lead to problems in the relationship. Marriage is not a game of give-and-take. It's a very serious step. It's a lifetime of commitment, something that takes time, energy, obligation, and dedication. When one enters into marriage, it is your moral responsibility to be the best you can be in the relationship, enhancing one another. Never enter into a relationship where you're not committed to enhancing one another. You improve, strengthen, and bring out the worth and beauty of each other.

Paul says, as God has distributed to each one, as the Lord has called each one, so let him walk. 1 Corinthians 7: 17 KJV. The apostle Paul was instructing the church on marital issues within the churches, teaching them to let each one seek to conduct and regulate their affairs as so to lead the life which the Lords has allotted and imparted to them and to which God has invited and summoned them. In our society, not only is there a high rate of divorces outside of the church, the rate for divorced couples within the church is rising to a predictable high proportion. Each individual has the potential to change the atmosphere around him or her. Couples are so quick to find blame in the other mate when, in actuality, there are times when the person doing the complaining needs prayer. There comes a point in every relationship in which individuals consider, evaluate, and examine themselves, judging and asking themselves what values or qualities they are bringing into the relationship.

God has a way of showing us ourselves so we may make the correct adjustments within our lives and the lives of those around us, for example, being honest when it comes to our shortcomings, admitting to each other when were wrong, and correcting the incorrect. The power of forgiveness, having the ability to being able to forgive someone who has offended you, is about coming to the marriage table together, expressing to each other the need to communicate to effectively resolve issues. Cultivating your relationship makes sure it grows properly. You want your relationship to be beneficial mentally, physically, and spiritually.

SEX AND MARRIAGE

Did you know that when God ordained the bonds of marriage, he gave legal sanction. He blessed the relationship between a man and a woman. It was an established ceremony between two people who were both joined together in holy matrimony, God was presiding priest and judge, and it was all good in God's eyesight. When God created man, it was a good thing, and when God created woman, it was an extraordinary thing. God implemented various laws when it came to sexual morality. God implemented certain laws that were forbidden, clarifying and explaining in details the rules of sexual conduct. Leviticus 18 states that none of you shall approach any who is near of kin to uncover their nakedness. It was forbidden to lay with your father, mother, or sister. Even if she were born to the father from another relationship, it was forbidden. Also included was a grandchild, your daughter's daughter, an aunt, uncle, a brother's wife, a woman's daughter, a son's daughter, or your neighbor's wife. It was forbidden for:

- A man to have sex with a woman during her monthly visitation
- A man to have sexual relations with another man the same as with a woman
- A man and woman to have sexual relations with animals
- A man to commit adultery with another man's wife and was punishable by death (Lev. 20: 10)

There were no restrictions when it came to the bonds of marriage between a husband and wife. "Marriage should be honored by all, and the marriage bed kept pure, for God will judge the adulterer and all the sexually immoral" (Heb. 13:4 NIV). This means having sex was legal. It was a sacred ceremony for the married couples. The marriage was honorable in all, meaning they were clean in everything. In the eyes of God, the bed was undefiled.

In many of the letters to the church, Paul dealt with certain issues regarding marriage relationships. In 1 Corinthians 7:1–17,Paul states, "[N]ow I will cover the things you wrote to me concerning." Paul goes on to instruct the church to avoid fornication, that is, having sexual relations with someone not married to you.

Paul states that, if you find yourself in an unholy situation, let every man have his own wife and let every woman have her own husband. "The husband should fulfill his marital duty to his wife, and likewise the wife to her husband" (1 Cor. 7:3 NIV). The

Bible is filled with information when it comes to the marriage relationship and how couples are to conduct themselves. One of the most romantic chapters in the Bible is the Song of Solomon, where he goes into detail expressing his love for his spouse, which can be found all throughout the verses of chapter 4. Throughout the entire book of Solomon, he describes love, faith, and desire, just as Christ loved the church and gave his life for it.

To talk about sex in the church today has almost become a taboo. We go to counseling for marital problems. We attend marriage conferences, we buy books and tapes on marriage, and every issue pertaining to marriage is covered except sexual conduct between married couples. Why do we decline such topics when it comes to the subject as to why couples are having problems in the privacy of their bedroom? If the world can talk about sexual issues, why can't the church be open-minded, too?

I think it's time to talk about sex. Scripture fills the Bible regarding how married couples are to engage themselves when it comes to sexual pleasures. For most couples, sex is a nuisance and, in some cases, creates problems within the relationship. I recently came across an article of the top five complaints husbands have toward their wives.

1. Husbands admitted their frustrations with their wives' appearance, anywhere from waking up in the morning to retiring for the night. Their wives were a total turnoff.
2. Husbands complained that their wives spent all day walking around the house in a robe and a head full of rollers.
3. Many men complained about the house not being clean and dinner not being on the table in a timely

manner when they arrived home from work. Instead, their wives spent hours gossiping over the phone and being busybodies.

4. Men complained their wives had no sex life, with no excitement and no creativity.

5. Men complained that their wives spent more quality time engaging themselves in other things rather than spending quality time together. They complained their wives were burnt out when it came to engaging in sex.

In the earlier chapters, I covered how cultivating your marriage is so essential to the relationship. It also includes your sexual relationship as well. God created sex for the married. It is to be a mutual exchange between a man and a woman, engaging in the pleasure of love. It's sharing tender affections toward one another, having strong romantic sexual desire for your own mate. Sex is something you don't give up on unless there is a health issue that prohibits one from performing. Just as you cultivate other areas in your relationship, it's about improving and developing your love life as well.

I observed Christian couples in the church and how they engage so much of their time in the activities of the church. You wonder when they find the time to spend quality time with each other. Centering yourself around the church all the time is not what I would describe as couples' quality time. It's taking the time to spend the time, just the two of you together engaging in a nice, quiet evening enjoying one another.

In some relationships, the desire to have sex has almost faded away over the years. It has gone from every other night to once a week to once or twice a month, which can create a strain in a marriage. There could be a number of reasons for such a breakdown. Some couples admit they don't have the time to plan a nice romantic evening with their busy schedules trying to work and raise children. Perhaps it's insecurity about your weight. You don't feel as attractive as you once did. Anger and frustration could also kill the desire for sexual pleasure. Anger can be expressed loudly, and desires can diminish. Anger is an action word, and it can be expressed in many ways. Anger and frustration can dismantle a marriage in a matter of months. Especially in those troubled times, a bed divided cannot stand. Making the wrong statement at the wrong time will result in no playtime at bedtime.

Children have a way of keeping your life occupied with no time to get sexy and have fun, so when it comes down to having sex, it's all about getting a quickie before the kids wake up, a temporary solution that will last for a limited time. Having sex can become a weekend planner or Friday nights only. With work and children, the word called "timeout" is translated to the expression, "You just don't want to be bothered." Nowadays, roles are shifting from husband and wife to mom and dad. Children have a misconception that moms and dads do not have sex. They think sex is something that flew out of the window the moment they were conceived. Even for parents to mention the "S" word is a taboo.

The relationship can be rejuvenated with just a few simple steps. Lack of desire doesn't mean:

- Your marriage is on the brink of disaster.
- You're not attracted to your spouse.
- You have to throw in the towel.

It just means that you need to give more attention to your relationship and cultivate the intimacy you once enjoyed together. It takes two to tango, and it will take the both of you working together to regenerate each other's passion and the emotions you once shared. Spending quality time together is essential to any marriage relationship. It connects your spirits together, along with the gift of touching, which can work wonders. Physical contact can stir sexual desires. Sharing a good massage together can be therapeutic and relaxing. Embrace each other affectionately, put your arms around your mate's body, and hold each other tightly just to show affection and pleasure. Gently kiss one another. The gift of touch can make a difference in a relationship.

What do you do when you feel like the thrill is gone? What happens when you're not in the mood to be romantic and you don't have a desire for having sex? Sex is all part of marriage. You can't have one without the other, and I advise you sit down and figure out how you can both spend quality time together. For some, having sex should not be done at the spur of the moment. There should be a preparation of working up to the moment: courting, spending time together to romance one another, kissing and touching each other, laughing with each other, or sharing a bite of strawberries dipped in chocolate. It all revolves around working your way up to that moment.

Don't be so preoccupied with other things that you ignore the needs of your partner. This is not the will of God. "The wife has not power of her own body but the husband and likewise the husband has not power of his own body but the wife" (1Cor. 7:4–5)."Defraud not one another" means not depriving your mate of sex. Don't cheat him or her of what belongs to him or her. Don't say you're on your monthly visitation when you're not.

It's just your excuse for not having sex. If it's not a good time, then gently sit down and explain why you feel the way you do and reschedule another time. It may work for some men, but for other men, it won't, especially when they have been deprived for weeks. The Bible goes on to say in the very same verse, "Defraud you not one another except for a time that you may give yourselves to fasting and prayer and come together again that Satan tempt you not."

When intimacy is ignored in the bedroom, in some cases, it gives the other mate reasons to have extramarital affairs. I advise you don't create a problem where it doesn't have to be one. Make time for each other. Try making a change in the performance. Do something different. It's good to be creative as long as both partners have given their consent. As long as your partner isn't tying you up, spanking you, hanging you from the ceiling, having rough sex, or having sex with any animals, relatives, or another man's wife, whatever you and your mate consent to do together in the privacy of your own bedroom is not a sin. In a marriage relationship, the bed is undefiled. If your mate wants to kiss and lick you from your head all the way down to your toes, it should be a pleasure. If he delights in the pleasure of your breast, Solomon said two breasts are like young roes and clusters of grapes (Song of Sol. 7:37). The Song of Solomon gives us a taste of how a man should look upon the woman he loves. Solomon shares his desire and delights. He enjoys the pleasure of his wife. Solomon was a poet of love.

Get rid of the kids for the weekend. Send them packing with family or friends. Bring something fresh to the bedroom. Set a table for two with a candlelit dinner .Spray the rooms with different, sweet-smelling perfumes. Set the atmosphere with romantic music, music that brings back memories, like a little Marvin Gaye, Luther Vandross, or Barry White, to name a few. It wouldn't hurt a bit to "turn out the lights and light a candle," as Teddy Pendergrass suggested. Perhaps jazz is your pleasure. Others prefer a little Frank Sinatra. "Amazing Grace" and "Jesus Keep Me Near the Cross" would not be one of my selections when I'm spending a romantic evening with just my baby and me.

Ladies, try something different for a change. Get out of those tired, faded pajamas. Take a trip to the lingerie department. Explore all of your options, and shop around for something sexy, something that will knock your mate off his feet. If your mate is not the type who shops for himself, make your way over to the men's department and pick him up a pair of silk satin pajamas.

Use your imagination to make the evening a pleasurable one. To the married, God has given you a gift. Marriage is honorable, blessed, and undefiled, and you have been given license to drive as long as both partners agree and it does not bring harm or discomfort to each other. When was the last time you and your partner just laid across the bed naked in the embrace of one another's arms? Genesis 2:24 says that Adam and Eve were both naked and not ashamed. The embrace of one another can bring closeness. You could fall asleep in one another's arms. You can revive the passion. Don't preoccupy yourselves with other things to the point you neglect your marriage relationship. Don't be so spiritual-minded, so spiritually deep, that you are no earthly good. There is a time and season for everything under the sun, and each has its own place. There is a time to be spiritual, and there is a time to be in the natural.

It really boggles my mind to see so many Christian couples having marital problems. You're asking God to enlarge your territories for spiritual desires, but while you're praying, also ask God to enlarge your territories in the area of your love life as well. Then you will have balance in all areas of your life spiritually as well as naturally. God implemented the sexual relationship as a means of two people coming together and expressing their love for one another. Lovemaking should be pleasurable, satisfying, and delightful. It should not feel like you're being raped. It takes two people consenting together to engage in sexual pleasures.

There is a problem when married Christian couples can't come together to express their love to one another. As you get older, especially when the children are all grown and leave home, it should kick your love life up another notch. If you are having problems in the bedroom, ask God to revive your relationship. The Bible says that God also helps those who help themselves. There are so many things to choose from that will help you achieve the heights that you desire in the privacy of your bedroom, for example, different vitamins. You don't have to go to an X-rated store to find what you need. You can choose from so many things in your local department stores. It's all about using your imagination and being creative.

Some couples don't need help at all, and that's great, but for those of you who do, there is always help if you need it. If you want a happy, healthy relationship in all the areas of your marriage, invest into the things that are important to you. Take the time to care for what's important to you, keeping your relationship cultivated and full of excitement. Sex doesn't have to be boring. You can put the excitement back into your relationship when you are both working together to fulfill each other's pleasures. Remember, you have a license that means you're legal. You have a permit from God. He has authorized sex for the married. You both have permission to have fun in your bed. There are no restraints when it comes to sex. It's all good in God's eyesight, so do it until you're satisfied.

NO COMPARISON; YOU'RE YOU

Each and every one of us is created differently. Even down to our fingerprints, no two people are alike. God made each of us in his own image. That's why everyone is entitled to his or her own opinion. Imagine what the world would be like if everyone agreed on the same things. It wouldn't leave room for imagination or expression. In marriage, couples do not think alike. They don't look alike, dress alike, and talk alike simply because they are different. Some women don't appreciate the freedom their husband gives to them, and they will take advantage of that liberty, for example, going out with their girlfriends and coming home in the late hours of the evening. You are actively involved in social gatherings, church functioning's, and being present every time the doors of the church open in the midst of being involved with everybody else. You neglect quality time you can spend with your own family.

I was the perfect example of not taking time to spend with my family. I was actively involved in our church activities. I was choir president music director, church secretary and actively involved in the women's department. I was the Sunday school teacher for the youth. I was present when the pastor called for weekly revivals. I had to be present for monthly district meetings. I attended church musicals and as if my busy schedule were not enough. I was actively involved with the ministers' wives board. I was pulled in all sorts of directions. It was a small church, and I was the pastor's daughter-in-law. I made time for everyone and everything else, but I ignored the needs of my own children. We never left our children at home. They were always in church with us. Wherever I was, my children were always right there with me, but I never stopped to ask how they were feeling about being so actively involved in the things I was doing.

My husband's agenda was the same as mine. He was a minister, and his schedule kept him on the go with preaching engagements. He was president of the men's department. He was Bible teacher on Tuesday evenings. His schedule was just as demanding as mine. I did not notice it at the time because I was so caught up in the moment of the activities of the church, but my husband began to notice the children's behavior, like their grades beginning to drop, among other things.

It was making a strain on our family. Church had become a chore to them, a task, a routine that had become boring to them. My husband had to stop and evaluate our priorities. He decided to reduce some of our church activities and focus our attention more on our family. I must admit that I did not initially agree with giving up some of my responsibility to someone else in the church, but as time passed, I could see the importance of quality time with my children.

Our children's grades began to pick up, and my husband and I had more time to spend together. I look back now, and I really regret not being present for their sports activities. My son played football. I missed the opportunity of not seeing him run the ball, and he missed seeing his mama on the stands cheering. I missed my daughter running track, playing basketball, and cheerleading. There is nothing more rewarding than to see your children achieve and develop into their full potential. I always wondered what if I had pushed my children in the sports they were so good at, and possibly they could have achieved a professional career in the sports they loved so dearly.

God is concerned about the whole family, not just the four corners of the church walls. It is God's desire that the whole family be saved. Just as you spend quality time in the church and other activities, give your family that equal amount of time. God does not expect you to give your best to the church and neglect your own family. Why not give your best equally to both?

Ladies, there is a difference between being single and being married. When you are single, meaning you are unmarried without a spouse or unattached, you don't have a deadline to meet. You answer for your own self. When you're married, meaning there is not only one space but two, you're no longer your own boss. Now you're in the position to answer to someone else. You can't hang out with your girlfriends all day and most of the evening because they are single and you're not. You can't just jump in the car and say, "I'll be back whenever." Your girlfriends may have a man who doesn't care that they go out and stay out until the wee hours of the morning, or they may not have a man at all.

Your main concern should be taking care of what you have at home because there is unity when the home is in order. You have some women who are busy bodies. The Bible talks about those busybodies. They are up in everyone else's business but their own. 1 Timothy 5: 13, NIrV, says they get into the habit of having nothing to do. They go around from house to house. They waste time. They talk about others. They bother people. They say things they shouldn't say.

Men and women, what attracted you to your spouse? When we entered into our relationship, we paid more attention to the superficial. Some of us looked at what was on the surface instead of inner qualities. Things will change. With time, nothing stays the same forever. If your woman has a brick house body or your

man looks like he just stepped off the cover of *GQ*, enjoy it while
you can because he will not look that way forever. With time, as
the song goes, what goes up must come down. We all have found
something in our mates that we fell in love with, whether it
was their smile, laugh, or thoughtfulness. Whatever the reasons
you fell in love with your mate, bring out the best in him or
her. Never try to mold him or her into someone else's image.
There is nothing wrong with trying to improve your mate for
the better, but you must give him or her space at expressing who
he or she is. If you pattern yourself like others, the real you will
not be visible. You would have created an imitation of someone
else. After a while, you will find yourself walking and talking,
mimicking other people's characters.

God gives you your own individuality, which specifically
distinguishes you from anyone else. God has imparted gifts
within each and every one of us. There is nothing like being
you! You will never begin to develop your God-given potential
because you are imitating someone else's gift and not your own.
You are an original blueprint. There is no one who can display
you better than you.

Husbands never compare your mate to your mother and
make statements like, "I wish you were like my mother ... I wish
you could cook the way my mother cooks." You might just find
yourself walking into a lion's den. On the other hand, wives, be
careful when you say things like, "I wish you were more like my
daddy ... I wish you were like him or her."

When my husband and I first got married, he would always
make statements like, "I wish you could do this or that like my
mama ... I wish you could cook like my mama." My husband's
mother was an excellent homemaker. You name it, she could do
it and did it well. She would make the best pancakes. However,

when I attempted to make pancakes, they turned out black on both sides, looking like the map of Texas instead of being round. Breakfast was always a total disaster for me, but nothing more would make me angrier than when my husband compared me to his mother. I felt it was so unfair for him to do this. His mother had years in the business of being a homemaker. She had raised five children. How could he begin to compare the two together?

It was like running a marathon. The moment I got into position to run my relay, she was already at the finish line. Perhaps your mate is not like your mother, but give her a little time and patience. She will eventually learn, and with time and support from you, it all goes back to what to look for in a mate. If food is your thing, you will want to find a woman who can cook. Ladies, if cooking is your weakness, you need to enroll in some cooking classes. Take it from me. A man loves good cooking!

You bring out the best in each other and give each the freedom to express what's inside him or her. It's not all about you, yourself, and you. It's about the both of you pulling out those gifts God has ordained in the both of you. And when God saw, what he had created, it was all good. Did you not know that you are to minister to one another's needs?

Ladies, you say you want to be a minister, right? It's your desire to travel the world and evangelize the nations, but did you know your first ministry starts at home? Brothers, you want to grab your briefcase and Bible, attend book engagements around the world, and minister to the need of others, but you neglect your own family's needs. In order to be an effective minister, it starts first at home ministering to the needs of your own family. How can you care for the needs of other people and neglect your own family?

Ministry first starts at home. If the home is well organized, then God can trust you when it comes to the organization of his church, for example, how you treat people and how well you communicate with others when you don't always agree with what they do. When you are building on a solid foundation, you will never know what kind of jewel you have until you uncover what's buried deep down inside in your own backyard.

HE'S NOT YOUR DADDY; HE'S YOUR LOVER

When I was growing up as a child, I had a wonderful relationship with my adopted father. I was Daddy's little girl. I looked up to him. He was my hero. He represented everything a father was supposed to be. I always felt protected when he was around. Walter Clark was the perfect father in my eyesight. He loved and nurtured me. I had a close relationship with my mother, but I had a bond with Daddy.

Daddy worked hard to try to provide all of my needs. I didn't lack anything. I had all sorts of pretty little dresses with the lace socks and shoes to match. I was Little Miss Sunshine.I had nothing but the best.

One summer, Daddy bought this big backyard swimming pool. I invited all of my little friends over to play in the pool. By the end of the evening, all the kids from the neighborhood were in my backyard.

I always looked forward to my birthday and Christmas, which both fell in the same month. They were very special occasions. My mother would plan the best birthday parties. We always had a house full of kids at my birthday parties. I would especially enjoy the two birthday cakes I would get every year, one from my mother and the other from Aunt Doris. She would make my favorite, German chocolate. Birthday presents were everywhere. I especially liked the birthday cards with money in them. Daddy would stand there with a big grin as I opened up each present.

Christmas was a special occasion. Daddy always made the holidays feel festive. Daddy would bring the Christmas tree and decorations down from the attic, and we would decorate the house. Music was always in the air in our home. Daddy's favorite songs were "White Christmas" by Bing Crosby and "The Christmas Song (Chestnuts Roasting on an Open Fire)"by Nat King Cole.

Weeks before Christmas, I would make my list and check it twice and address my mail to the North Pole. I would wait for the mail carrier to arrive to make sure he got my message to Santa. I always wondered why Mama would ask me what was on my list. I would discover the reason as I got older. They would rush me off to bed on Christmas Eve with a glass of milk and a handful of cookies. I would try to stay awake to make sure Santa didn't forget anything on my list, but my sleepy eyes wouldn't hear of it. The next morning, I would awake bright and early, run to the Christmas tree, and look in amazement at all the presents that lay under the Christmas tree. Everything on my list was under the shimmering Christmas tree.

One of the most tragic times in my life was the day Daddy died. I would wake up every morning and greet Mama and Daddy good morning. Mama always had breakfast prepared. I would get dressed for school and bid them both good-bye. On my way out the door, I would holler to Daddy, "I'll see you when you get home. I love you, Daddy."

Daddy drove trucks for a living and normally arrived home just in time to tuck me in bed. It was my first year in junior high. I was excited because I had finally made it out of elementary school. I felt like a big girl now. Daddy and Mama would take turns driving me to school, but I wanted to be like all the other kids in the neighborhood and ride the school bus. Daddy would not hear of it. He was so overprotective of me, but with a little begging, he finally gave in. One morning, I noticed Daddy following the bus to make sure I got to school safely.

This particular morning was a normal routine. I kissed both Mama and Daddy good-bye and headed off for school. I couldn't wait to get home to see what delicious dish Mama was cooking for dinner. A group of my friends and I got off the bus and headed for home, laughing and joking with one another as usual. Our house was the second one from the corner of Sewanee Street. I could see cars parked at my house a block away, and it was unusual to have a crowd during the weekdays unless someone was visiting from out of town. I hurried home to see what the big excitement was all about and who our visitor was. Uncle Wesley (Mama's brother) greeted me first. I adored Uncle Wesley. He was always cheerful. He used to call me Pee Wee because I was so small and skinny. Uncle Wesley would always come to the rescue whenever I needed a tooth pulled as a child.

I had the greatest uncles and aunts. Uncle Wesley would escort me down the aisle on my wedding day. For some unusual reason, he had a sad expression on his face this particular day. He told me to hurry in the house because Mama was waiting for me. Hurrying into the house, I noticed everything looked so dark. The curtains were pulled, and that was unusual during the day. Relatives and friends filled the room. They all looked so sad. Everything looked gloomy.

Mama got up from where she was sitting, took me by the hand, and led me to one of the bedrooms. "Linda, there is something important I have to tell you."

I knew something was wrong, and it wasn't good.

"We had to rush Daddy to the hospital this morning because he got really sick."

I immediately interrupted, "Take me to the hospital so I can see Daddy. I will make him feel better."

I just rambled on until Mama interrupted me, "Honey, Daddy had a serious heart attack."

I looked at the sadness across her face. "Is he going to be okay?"

Mama pulled me closer to her and gave me a hug I will never forget as tears rolled down her face. "Linda, Daddy died on the way to the hospital."

Nothing could have ever prepared me for such a blow. I could not believe the word that was coming out of Mama's mouth. Everything became a daze to me. The tears began to roll down my face uncontrollably. I didn't want to believe my daddy was dead. The tears would not stop flowing. I cried for my daddy for days. He left and never said good-bye.

People would begin to fill our home, coming in and out, giving their condolences, and bringing all sorts of food. All kinds of delightful dishes filled our kitchen. I didn't have much of an appetite to eat. Family and friends brought flowers and shared a laugh, tear, or some memories. People shared their stories of how Mr. Clark touched their lives in so many ways.

The day we had to go view Daddy's body at Lewis Funeral Home, I couldn't stand the thought, but Mama said she needed me. She said she couldn't do this by herself. Only six months earlier, her mother, Grandma Henrietta, had died. Now Daddy was gone.

Mama tried to stay strong for me, but I knew she was hurting, too. The ride to the funeral home seemed like an eternity. I walked slowly into the room as the funeral director escorted us to the room where Daddy laid. As we approached the room, I could see a man in the coffin. I could not believe my eyes. There Daddy lay in a casket, dressed in a suit. Daddy never wore suits. His favorite attire was khaki pants or overalls. Daddy was not a member of anyone's church, but his mother Mittie was a devout Christian. She always looked like she was going to church. I often wondered if she were in the Pentecostal movement because I never saw her wear pants or makeup. Daddy wouldn't attend church, but he would always send his offerings by Mama. He would sit on the porch listening to the church services. Sometimes I would ask Mama if I could stay home with Daddy on Sundays, but she would not hear of it. Daddy always said he did not want to be a hypocrite. He didn't want to pretend to be something he wasn't. But I know he believed in God. At times, I would hear him weeping whenever Mama would play gospel songs.

We stayed right across the street from the church. The same people he would see at the juke joint on Saturday night, drinking, dancing, and cussing would be the same people sitting in church on Sunday morning shouting. He would always say that, if he ever stepped foot in the church, it would be when they rolled him down the aisle. And the only times I ever remembered Daddy stepping foot in a church was when his mother and Grandma Henrietta died. Six months later, they rolled Daddy down the aisle.

I still could not bring myself to grips that the man lying in the casket was my daddy. I sat in the chair and watched him for what seemed like hours. I watched the mourners come and go, but my eyes stayed on Daddy.

Mama touched me on the shoulder. "Baby, it's time to go home."

I didn't want to leave Daddy by himself at the funeral home, but Mama persuaded me to come with her. We headed home. The next day, I would sit in my bedroom window and watch them carry Daddy's casket into the church. After the memorial service, we went to the cemetery. I watched as they lowered his body into the ground. Something died inside of me the day they buried my daddy. I was angry with God and could not understand why he would take my daddy away from me. How could God make such a mistake?

Months and years went by. I never stop missing my daddy. I miss him to this very day, and a special place will always be in my heart for him. I had to come to understand that God allows things to happen in our lives, just as in the case with Job who lost everything he ever possessed—his cattle, children, and health. God allowed Satan to take everything that Job possessed except for a nagging wife. Job knew that, in spite of the mishaps, God was in total control of his life, so Job never lost focus on the things of God. He declared, Though he slay me, yet will I trust him Job 13:15 KJV

When I got married, I expected my husband to also provide the things my father provided for me. My expectations were stacked high. I expected my husband to fill the voids that Daddy left behind. It became a burden that complicated our relationship early in our marriage. My husband did his best to provide for me. We both dropped out of high school to get married at an early age, he being sixteen and I being seventeen. The job market was small considering our age and our educational background .Opportunities were limited. My husband was hired for menial jobs that paid less. I was hired as a waitress at a local restaurant, which was cut short due to the birth of our first child. I expected too much from my husband who only had limited resources at the time. I was trying to pull something out of him that was only found in Daddy.

I would make statements like, "If Daddy were here, he would do things like this … Why can't you be more like my daddy? You can't tell me what to do. You're not my daddy."

I had to learn that God had placed Daddy into my life for such a time. God knew what I needed, lots of love and attention. Five years before Daddy died, I would find out that Mama and Daddy were not my biological parents. In fact, they were my distant uncle and aunt. Mama could not have children of their own, and I was their answered prayer. These two incredible people adopted me when I was two. I was a very sickly child, just skin and bones as an infant. The doctors said I wouldn't live to see my fifth birthday, and if I did, I would have physical problems for the rest of my life. They had faith that God was a miracle worker. I had problems walking. I wore braces on both of my legs until I was five. I was their little miracle baby.

It amazes me that God allowed me to remember when I was an infant about two year old. Daddy and Mama would place a towel on this table and lay me on it. Daddy would rub me from head to toe with olive oil. I once told Daddy what I remembered. I asked him why he had to put so much oil on me. I looked like a greased chicken sitting up on the table. He would laugh and say the olive oil was healing oil. They cared and loved me as if I were their own child. They protected me from any negative talk. My adoption was a well-kept family secret. I would later find out that Grandma Henrietta was actually my great-great-great grandmother and Aunt Irene was my great-great grandmother (Mama's sister).The pretty lady who would often come from New Jersey for a visit was actually Grandmother Rose. When I was a child, Mama had a picture of this beautiful woman posed in a swimsuit. She looked like a supermodel. She was so beautiful. I would later discover the lady in the picture was my birth mother. It was a well-kept family secret that no one talked about. My adopted parents spent thousands of dollars on me. I was in and out of the hospital until I was ten. They probably would have never told me about the adoption if I had not been sneaking around in their private papers and found a copy of my adoption papers. Mama said they would have eventually told me when the time was right. They didn't want to do anything to cause me pain.

Once I got over the initial shock of them not being my biological parents, I was amazed as to why my own flesh and blood parents didn't fight to keep me, along with my three other siblings who other family members raised. I would later find out my mother was just a teenage girl when she gave birth to me. She was asked to sign papers, not knowing she was actually signing her own child away. It was my mother's understanding that we would stay temporarily with relatives until she recovered from her illness and her children would be returned to her. Little did she know that her child would belong to someone else and she couldn't do anything about it because she signed her name on the dotted line.

But God had a purpose and plan for my life. I had to realize Daddy was now gone and would no longer be a part of my life, but his spirit would always be with me. I also had to realize that it was unfair for me to expect my husband to take his place. I had to learn to leave my past behind and cherish the memories. Matthew 19:5, KJV saysFor this reason a man shall leave his father and mother and be joined to his wife and the two shall be one flesh. God began to heal the wounds in my life that my father's death left.

In the midst of the confusion, I came to know Jesus in a special way. He healed the hurting times. God healed the anger that I carried within me for so many years.

Ladies, don't expect your husband to be like your daddy. Your husband is not your daddy. He's your lover. He is there to love and cherish you. He picks up the pieces where your father leaves off. Your husband will fulfill things in your life your father could never. Give him a chance to show what he can be to you. Perhaps he's not everything you desired him to be, but stand by his side and push him to be the best he can be. Stop looking at what the Jones have and appreciate the things you have. Work toward goals you wish to achieve in life. So many people look at the achievement of others, and they fail to recognize what it cost others to live the way they do. They may have it all—the home, car, and money in the bank—but their home is out of control. The husband may work two and three jobs, and the wife may work just as many jobs in order to pay the bills to live the type of lifestyle they desire. But they can't see eye to eye on anything.

Their children are in shambles, looking for love in all the wrong places. It's all because no one has time for the children. Mama and Daddy are so busy working to maintain their busy lifestyles, and they have lost focus on what's really important in life. Material things cannot substitute for a loving, well-balanced family. People will only reveal a piece of a picture, the part they want everyone to see. They won't reveal the problems in the home. They want everyone to see their one big, happy family.

If you live in a little one-bedroom apartment and you pay your bills each month, you have a roof over your head, food to eat, and clothes on your back. You're not always fussing and cussing. Smile and be happy. Don't expect the world when he can only give you him for the time being. Stand by a good man, not the ones who lay up all day waiting for someone else's paycheck to pay the bills and put food on the table. I'm talking about a good, hardworking man who will bust his behind to provide for his family. A good man's change will come. He will fulfill your dreams, hopes, and desires. A good man will not withhold one good thing from you. He will give to you more than what you ask for. He will fulfill areas in your world, more than what your father could. He's your friend, partner, and lover, and he's your man.

PART THREE

MARRIED WITH CHILDREN

A television sitcom called "Married with Children" is about a dysfunctional family of four. The father Al works as a local shoe salesman who feels like life forgot him along the way. He feels like all of his dreams have been shattered as a result of getting married and having children. He blames his wife Peg for some of his misfortunes. Al hates his job, and he tries to improve on some things in life but lacks the necessary job skills. Al, at times, seems to have forgotten his purpose in life. He focuses more on what could have been rather than seeking ways to improve the family's future. Peg is a couch potato, a bored desperate housewife who lives in a time capsule from the sixties. Peg tries to put things in the right perspective, but she lacks skills in the homemaking department.

Both Al and Peg lack skills in the parenting department. Peg seeks ways to put spice back into the marriage, but Al thinks his world stopped rotating at thirty. They have two dysfunctional teenagers, Kelly and Bud. Kelly, their daughter, looks for love in all the wrong places, and Bud, their son, will do anything just to draw attention. Let's not forget the family pet that seems to be more intelligent than them all.

Perhaps your family isn't as dysfunctional as the Bundy household is, but most people tend to agree that everything changes when children come into the picture. Your honeymoon house will shortly become an extended family household. The moment children enter the scene; your life takes on a completely different world. Those plans you have made for the future will soon take a temporary backseat. You're no longer your own, your life will take a detour, and your plans are no longer centered around you and your mate. Life takes on a whole new meaning. It's now centered around your newfound family. You're now married with children, which are little blessings sent down from above and, at times, can actually be a rewarding experience.

I became pregnant three months after my husband and I were married. We were young and naïve, unaware of what lay ahead for our future. When the nurse first put my son in my arms, he was the most adorable baby I had ever laid my eyes on. I couldn't believe that this child was an actual product of my husband and me. We really had good chemistry, but in the midst of me bonding with this tiny bundle of joy, all of a sudden, fear shadowed my thinking. I had just bargained for something I had no knowledge of. It became so overwhelming that I suddenly realized that I was now a mother and I had the responsibility to do everything in my power to love and protect this small bundle of joy. I wanted to be the best mother I could be. I was driven to be a good mother, a drive I had within myself that I had to get it right, no matter what. I knew nothing about being a mother. Mama took really good care of me, but now the shoe was on the other foot, mine. I had carried this child inside of me for nine whole months, a miracle in itself of how a woman can carry another living human being inside of her womb for this time. It's truly one of the mysteries of God. No man can do what a woman was created to do best; no woman can do what a man was created to do best. When God created woman, she was a gem. She was created to be valuable, useful, and beautiful. She had no need for makeup. Her beauty was her glory.

I went through all the stages of pregnancy with flying colors except for the leg cramps, which I didn't particularly care for. To describe the labor is another story. It was physically hard work, and it took every ounce of my strength to get the job done. It was a process. Nothing happened quickly. Everything seemed to go in slow motion. The contractions were a process. It was a process of the tightening of my womb, and this tightness occurred frequently in painful intervals. I had never experienced pain so bad. No one prepared me for this kind of pain that lasted for twenty-four hours straight. No words describe what childbearing pain is all about, and for every pain that shot through my body, I remembered my husband. My personality went from a nice girl to the *Exorcist*. I lit up the labor and delivery room with my screaming and caused all the other mothers to begin screaming in harmony. My poor husband was confused. He didn't know whether to come or go. At first, I wanted him present during the whole birthing process. I wanted us to both see our bundle of joy come into the world, but when the pain started to move all over my mortal body, I wanted to crucify him. I blamed him for everything, for every pain that shot through my body. Why couldn't it have been him instead of me?

I thought to myself, *Why did Eve eat that apple? That heifer brought misery on all womankind.*

I shook the hospital bed. I pulled my hair. I tossed from one side of the bed to the other, trying to ease my pain, but no relief was in sight. There were no injections to relieve the pain, such as what we are so blessed to have today. I felt like something was happening that I could not control. I was a quiet, young woman, never trying to do anything to embarrass myself. Looking back at me then, I did not look like the same person twenty-four hours before. Sweat was running all over my face, and my hair was all over my head, looking like a nappy Afro. Between Mama and my husband, I didn't know who to strangle first. Mama was giving the doctors her motherly advice and recommended a Cesarean section, and upon learning what Mama was advising the doctors, I barred her from my room and then begged her back. Fifteen minutes later, we were both in tears.

I thought, *If only I had listened to Mama earlier in the day when I was eating that pot of mustard greens I had craved for two weeks.*

At first, I thought I had ate too many mustard greens, but when the pains started coming regularly, Mama knew I was in labor. I prolonged the time watching *All My Children*. I had to see if Jessie and Angie were going to get back together again. They finally got me to the car, and away we went to the hospital.

Well, after twenty-four long, agonizing hours, it was finally over. James Jr. was born at 6:10, weighing six pounds and eleven ounces. We were all so relieved that it was all over. I swore to God I would never have any more children after James Jr. was born, but I had three more beautiful daughters. The next time around, God gave me a break because giving birth to the girls was a breeze.

My husband and I did not realize we were both in for a rude awakening. Our family would soon become the Burley bunch. We had hands-on training when it came to parenting the basics 101 live and in living color.

I will share some of our experiences being young parents trying to raise children. I am so blessed to be a part of my children's lives. Each one of my children has different personalities. I am glad they are all so different. That makes them so special. I am blessed that God allowed me to be their mother. It has been a challenge but with every challenge comes reward. You will come to feel the same way when you stop and think about how your whole life has evolved around your children, and one day, you will recognize that your little babies are no longer babies, but now they have grown up to be fine, productive young adults. You will cherish the memories, especially in those quiet times. Invest your time and love into your children. Enjoy every moment you spend with your children because it will only be a memory one day.

OUR CHILDREN ARE OUR INVESTMENT FOR THE FUTURE

Children are an investment of the Lord. We are totally responsible for the molding and development of their lives. Our children are a product of our environment, and if you raise them on godly principles, they will grow up to be productive adults one day. Proverbs 22:6 says we should train up a child in the way he should go, and when he is old, he will not depart from it. It starts from the cradle, teaching our children godly principles, the power of prayer, and how to communicate with God and instilling the faith within them that God truly loves all of his children. It's powerful when we can pray with our children, that is, when we allow them to participate in our prayer time and teach them the guidelines of prayer.

By teaching them how to worship God, our children learn by imitating their parents. Take your children to church. Don't just send them, and as they get older, you would have instilled godly principles into their minds. They will never stray far from their teachings even as they face adulthood. Parents, realize you can't be in your children's life 24-7. When they begin to reach the age of puberty, the stage where they will began to develop physically and mentally, they will go through changes of maturity as they develop. They will experience pressures by their own peers, adopting certain behaviors and wanting to dress certain ways, and they will develop certain attitudes in order to be accepted as part of certain groups.

The power of prayer during those trying times can plant seeds into your child's life. Prayer can move mountains. Learn to be patient and calm when you're faced with making difficult decisions. Your child is developing an inquisitive mind. They're curious and eager for knowledge. And with instilling godly principles into your child at an early age, they will begin to know right from wrong. When relating to certain issues, they will have a moral sense of responsibility. If they stray, they will not go far. They will remember your teachings. They won't forget the times they heard you pray. They won't forget the times where they would see you praising God. They will know and come to recognize who their source is. When the storms of life come their way, they will remember the things they were taught. It's your responsibility to give good counsel to your children because they will remember your values somewhere down the line of their lives.

In the Old Testament, children were taught from an early age about the things of God. For the apostle Paul, his very first schooling was sitting at the feet of his parents. Then it was sitting at the feet of Rabbi Gamaliel. In Acts 22:3, Paul states he was a Jew born in Tarsus in a city in Cilcia and brought up in this city at the feet of Gamaliel, who taught him according to the perfect manner of the law of the fathers.

From a child listening to stories brought down to them from generation to generation, they were taught about the awesome power of God. They learned about Moses and how God used him to bring the children of Israel out the land of Egypt and how God used Moses to part the Red Sea so they might cross over to safety. They were familiar with King David and his son, King Solomon. They were taught these oral stories throughout their lives, and when they came of age, they had to learn the Torah, teachings of the Old Testament, the Books of the Law. Some children came from the tribe of Levi, which meant their fathers were responsible for temple duties. During those times, the role of the father was passed down to the son to inherit.

A long time ago, parents instilled values into their children. It was the father's responsibility to go out and work and bring in the paycheck. It was the mother's responsibility to make sure the home was comfortable and in order. She washed, ironed clothes, and cleaned the house. She made sure the children got off to school on time. She was PTA mom. She always hung around the school and kept in contact with your teachers to make sure you were doing the right thing. They all worked together. Everyone— the nosy neighbors, church members, and teachers—kept you in check. Everyone was up in your business.

Back in the day, it was not strange for neighbors, church people, and teachers to correct you for misbehaving. Just hope and pray they had mercy and didn't tell your parents about it. If your parents found out you were misbehaving, it was double your trouble when you got home. Your mother would lecture you for hours, and then you were paddled. Today, we live in a very different society. Parents won't let anyone correct their children, and many parents do not believe a word you say when it comes down to their children.

Parents, don't be so quick to say what your kids won't do. Nine times out of ten, your children will do what you thought they wouldn't do. And they will actually stand flat-footed, look you in your face, and tell a lie. Don't always be so quickly to believe that your child won't tell a lie. We lied to our parents, and your children will lie to you. My children would pull the wool over my head at times, and sadly, my husband knew when they were lying. I would not allow anyone to come to me and tell me my children were misbehaving, and when I would ask them concerning the matter, I would believe they would tell me the truth. I would be upset with anyone who challenged me or complained about my children. Come to find out, sometimes my children were the ones standing in the need of prayer and a good paddling. It wouldn't be until they were all grown and gone that they would confess jokingly how they told little lies so they wouldn't get in trouble. Parents, really get to know your children before you say what your child won't do because they just may surprise you.

In today's society, many parents don't spend quality time with their children. Many are too busy occupying themselves with other things, such as working two and three jobs to make ends meet, pursuing goals in Corporate America, or just working to provide the best for their children. Homemakers have turned in their aprons and dusters for briefcases. In our economy, you have both parents employed working full-time jobs, sometimes leaving their children home alone.

Single parents now have the responsibility of being the head of household. In 1977, statistics showed there were 119 million single parents with 84 percent of the children living with their mothers. It also revealed that 32 percent of the births were to unmarried women and 35 percent of parents were never married. The highest percentage of single parenting has risen to an astronomical rate, and the numbers continue to rise. The board of education have now adopted the role of helping to raise latchkey children by offering them after-school programs, tutoring sessions, and much more.

I had the opportunity a few years back to work with the school board, serving as a substitute teacher. I found out very quickly how and why some of the teachers have low morale. It is a very stressful but rewarding profession. Many teachers cannot handle the pressure that's placed on their shoulders on a daily basis. Many teachers retire early, or they just find other rewarding professions.

During my experience with the educational system, many children would come to school at times with bad hygiene. Their hair would not be combed. Their clothes looked as if they had just gotten out of bed. Many of the students were not prepared for class. They would show up with little or no school supplies. Some children hadn't had breakfast. Teachers became substitute parents as well as educators. We would wash their faces, comb their hair, ensure they had breakfast, and stay after class to assist them with their schoolwork. The teacher would go to the store to purchase school supplies on their lunch breaks because the children were not equipped with the necessary material for learning.

Most of the parents never maintained follow-ups on their children to check the progress of their academic work. Instead, parents would send notes with their children with excuses as to why their child was late or absent from school. Many of the children had so much anger built up on the inside of them that they would lash out at any and everybody. They did not understand how to focus their negative energy into a positive direction. They would fight with their schoolmates, their teachers, or the principal. They would start fights in the lunchroom. As a result of their behavior problems, their academic level was low. They failed to do their work in class and their homework, and at times, these children had to be sent home because they were out of control. I would not say that all of these children were bad children, as society would like to label them. These children were products of their own environments. They had issues at home. Many lacked the love, attention, and support that a child is supposed to have. They were always labeled as bad. I would hear some teachers tell the children they would not grow up to be anything because they were not willing to learn. They failed to have the compassion because they did not understand what was going on with the child, and many teachers failed in their arenas to take the time and give special attention to the child's needs.

These children did not understand how to express themselves. This was their way to vent their frustrations. They couldn't tell anyone they lived in an abusive home or their parents were alcoholic. They couldn't tell anyone that the only thing in their refrigerator was a picture of water. The welfare system would investigate those type of reports, and if the child were in an unhealthy environment, many children were removed from the home and placed in orphanages or foster care. These children did not want to be separated from their parents, no matter how bad the situation was.

I must admit there are teachers in the educational system who need other occupations. A majority of these teachers care nothing about the well-being of the child. For some of them, their only reason for coming to work is to collect a paycheck. Most of these teachers have lost their drive, focus, hunger, and motivation in the field of education. Some feel they have earned their education and it's up to the individual to strive to achieve his or her education. For some ethnic groups such as the African

American, Hispanic, and Native American low-income children, they unfortunately get the bad end of the stick.

On the other hand, some excellent teachers really love the children and care about the child's well-being. They will go the extra mile to make sure the child is equipped with the necessary tools to learn. These teachers will go over and beyond the call of duty to make sure this child achieves a quality education. I commend those teachers.

It is the parent's responsibility to take quality time to spend with children. Get up with your child. Prepare breakfast. If there are no bacon and eggs for breakfast, just get out of the bed to see them off to school and make sure they arrive early enough for the breakfast program at the building. Prepare them for this challenging world. Spend that quality time with them. Laugh and talk with them. Let them know you love them and you are concerned about the well-being of their lives. Walk them to the door, and let them see your smiling face before they head off to school. Start their morning off with a good day, and always tell your children you love them. That's important to know they're loved.

When our children were small, we didn't have much, but we had a lot of love, and we tried to provide for them the best we knew how. I would get up with my children, dress them, comb their hair, and walk or drive them to school. I would never let a day go by without telling my children how much I loved them.

I would always think to myself, *What if something would happen to me before the children got back home?*

Giving them a hug and kiss and saying "I love you" would have been the last words they would have heard me say. That was important they knew I loved them. My children are grown adults, and I still tell them I love them. Never let a day go by without telling your children how much you love them. It can make a difference in their lives.

We live in a generation that says, "It's your thing. Do what you want to do. Whatever makes you feel good, do it until you're satisfied." They say it's nobody's business but their own. They have no sense of responsibility. Many parents have lost their parental rights. They have lost their authority to exercise control over their children. Many parent use the cliché, "Don't do as I do; do as I say," but I am a firm believer that parents have to live by example. If you expect your children to obey and respect you, you have to be a worthy contributor. Live by example. Everyone can't be a parent. Just because you give birth to a child, that does not make you a mother. Respect is earned and not given. Be the type of role model your child can look up to.

How can you tell your children not to do certain things when you're doing the very same things yourself? How can you tell your daughters not to sleep around when you're slipping every Tom, Dick, and Harry into your home? You tell your children not to smoke when smoke fills your home. You tell your children not to drink alcohol, but they always see you popping open a Bud Light. You say bad habits are hard to break, and you don't want your children to pick up the same bad habits as you have. That's a good point. I couldn't agree with you more, but whatever you tell your children not to do, wouldn't you agree it all starts with you? You tell your children not to curse, but they hear you use swear words. You tell your children to forgive, but you won't.

How can they possibly respect the things you're telling them when you neglect to do them yourself? Live the life you tell others about. First remove the beam out of your own eyes before you tell someone else to remove the beam from theirs. If children can't confide in their own parents, then where do they turn? They will find attention in other people, places, and things, such as drugs, alcohol, gangs, and sex. Many children are lost. They don't know who they are because, at times, their parents have lost their own identity. This generation of children needs an outpouring of love and wisdom, and if the parents lack love, wisdom or knowledge, and purpose of who they are, then who will help the children?

When you begin to realize your worth, who you are, and who God says you are, then you can come to yourself and get yourself together. Then you can qualify yourself to impart wisdom into your child's spirit, along with the power of hope, the power to succeed, and the power to be great. Our children define themselves as GenX, but they do not comprehend what they are saying. They say it's because it sounds good. The X comes from Malcolm X. Malcolm had a reason for eliminating his last name and replacing it with an X.

Young people of today, if you're going to take on a symbol, be a part of an organization, grasp the meaning of its purpose, and be able to explain its roots of whatever cause you are standing for. If you stand, be willing to stand for something and understand what you are standing for, or else you will fall for anything.

Why did Malcolm change his name? His name was Malcolm Little. He felt it was the name of the plantation owner, a system that had enslaved his people for generations. The slaves were forced to adopt everything. They were forced to change everything about their culture and who they were as a people. Black people had a name before the *Mayflower*, and it was not their slave name. Rather than hold on to the name that had subjected his family to harsh and cruel domination, he chose to change his name from Malcolm Little to Malcolm X, meaning he had a name before the name Little and he did not know what that name was. It was not that he did not know who he was as a person. Malcolm knew who he was as a man, and he knew his purpose, but he had a name before the slave master gave him one.

After later traveling to Mecca, Malcolm discovered he was from the tribe of Shabazz, so now he became Malcolm Shabazz. People will say this generation is labeled Gen X because they don't know who they are. I say you must know where you come from in order to know where you're going. You must find out who you are and what you hope to be because you were born for a purpose. God created you for a purpose. There is a reason for your existence—not to kill each other, not to destroy your lives with drugs and alcohol, not to live your life out in the penal system, or not to destroy the gift God has so graciously created. We are all brothers and sisters. What is your purpose for killing each other? We all come from the same root.

My Native American, my African American, and my Hispanic and Latino brothers and sisters, we are all one. Read your history. It's time we come together and make peace. You were created to make a difference. You're not like none other, and you have a quality of being different in a positive way. You have the power to bring about positive change. You have the power to be great. Who are you, and what do you stand for?

Mothers teach your daughters not to sell themselves short. They don't have to prostitute themselves, degrade themselves, and be misused in order to gain something that's of no worth. Know and come to understand the meaning of true love. Love won't hurt. Mothers, teach your daughters they are gifts from God, they are queens, and they are the best of any kind. They are priceless, they are powerful, and they are God's best creation. It is important that our daughters know who they are before a man can define and abuse them.

Mothers, it's important to know who you are so you may impart good qualities into your daughters. My dear, sweet daughters, God has created you in his image. You were marvelously made, God has created you for excellence, and you were created to be outstanding and superior. God's gifts are stored within you. You're a jewel, a masterpiece created by God's own hands. You are special. You are worth waiting for, so don't sell yourself short for anything.

Fathers, instill into your sons who they are. They're not pimps, dope dealers, or dogs. Teach them their roles as young men. Teach them values of not trying to get over on the system, but to take full advantage of opportunity in a positive way. Teach your young men they were created to be strong and valiant. My sons, be men of honor, men of purpose. God has created you to be like the symbol of the eagle, a symbol of strength and power. You are the symbol of a lion, which represents bravery, fierceness, and admiration. You are to be celebrated. When God made man, he said, "Let us make man in our own image." In whose image? In the image of God.

Parents, if we don't tell our children who they are, they will not have a sense of direction or identity. They will be slaves to their own environment, passing their failures from one generation to another. If you do not tell them, they will look for affirmation in other places, thinking they have found the truth when, in actuality, they will find themselves caught up in a deadly deception.

Parents, never give up on your children. They will make mistakes. Their minds have not reached that mature stage in their live. Don't condone their wrongs. Tell them when they're wrong. Be careful of what you tell your children. It's important to speak positive words into their lives. Every child is born with a measure of potential. You were created to succeed, to become something. Perhaps your father and mother did not achieve some things in life and missed their opportunities. That does not mean they did not have potential. Somewhere down the line, they fell, and no one picked them up. Just because your father or mother may have failed, that does not label you a statistic, which does not mean your life has to fail as well.

Mothers, stop the cycle by telling your sons they will end up just like their no-good father. Fathers, stop the cycle by telling your daughters they will end up like their no-good mother. Because words are powerful, it is so vital to speak life into our children's spirit. The words you speak may determine that child's directions in life. Negative words can be damaging to a child's development because you define who they will be in a negative sense. These children will take those same negative words along with them into their adult life, feeling as if they are inferior to attain certain goals in their lives. Why? You have planted seeds that will produce a negative affect later in their lives. Let's help our children to be the best they can be. Plant positive seeds. Let them know they are special, they can be high achievers, and they have the potential to be leaders of the future.

Parents, get involved with your child's future. I believe that, if more parents got involved with the well-being of their children's education, there would be a lot less dropouts and teen pregnancies.

Compared to the time we were in school, our children have a lot more to contend with, namely peer pressure. In order to be accepted, you have to adopt a certain dress code, and if they do not dress a certain way, their peers reject them or make fun of them, which is an injustice and form of prejudice. Many young people are pressured because they cannot afford to wear designer clothing. Their peers mock and ridicule them. Many children are embarrassed to come to school because of the way they dress. They feel inferior to others who can afford to wear a certain style of clothes. They fail to miss the point. Their objective is not to look like a top fashion model. They should focus on trying to achieve a good education so that, in the future, they will have acquired the education they need so they may be hired for top-paying jobs. When you're getting paid well, you can afford to buy any clothing line you want.

As a result of these children focusing on the negative aspect, rather than ignore their peers for their ignorance, some of the brightest minds choose to drop out of school because of the peer pressure, which is a tragedy.

Then there is the other side of peer pressure. You have children whose parents are fortunate enough to buy their children designer clothing. Many are not designer clothes, but they look nice every time they come to school. They are ready to learn equipped with the supplies they need until they run into their jealous peers, so they are met with intimidation, violence, and blackmail, instilling fear into these children. These children have the mind-set to take something they have not earned so their peers can accept them, and as a result, the student who came prepared to learn is now discouraged and put his or her education at risk, all because of peer pressure.

When does the nonsense stop? In this generation, our children need all the help they can get because the next generation will be wild, suppressed, and uncontrollable, and if our children cannot find the support they need, they will discover it in other arenas. It's easy for our children to be hooked up with the wrong people. Trouble is easy to get into, but it's hard to get out of. Everyone who says their friends are not necessarily your friends do not have your best interest at mind. Our children yearn for a sense of belonging. If you ask a gang member why he joined a gang, he will tell you it's for acceptance. He will tell you they are family, they care about each other, they look out for one another, they will take a bullet for each other, or they will ride or die for each other. He will tell you he can be identified with something. He has a sense of belonging to someone or something. Everyone wants to be identified with something or someone, whether it is a social gathering, church, organizations, or sororities. You want to be identified with a group of people who share an interest concerning certain issues. So many of our youth join gangs as a sense of being identified or to belong somewhere. Did they wake up one morning and say, "I think I want to join a gang today" or "I think I want to be a thief and a robber" or "Perhaps I'll just go out and rape some women and children"? Did they wake up one morning and decide they wanted to be a serial killer? No, they didn't. It had to start from someone or somewhere. We have to question where the source came from. Was it the roots of discontent or feeling dissatisfied or unhappy about life? When did content transform itself into discontent? These things do not occur overnight. It is birthed from somewhere or someone.

When young people find themselves in gangs or other unhealthy situations, they are crying out for help. Some of their families are dysfunctional; some come from abusive homes. Their families are disconnected. They lack the love, attention, and sense of belonging they should have gotten at home. Instead, the streets become their family and a sense of belonging. They all have one thing in common. They are all hurting and trying to find healing. Nevertheless, in some cases, it's like the blind leading the blind, and eventually, they will all end up in a ditch drowning.

Some of these young men and women are bright young people. All they need is a chance and sense of direction. Many of these young people have the potential to work in Corporate America. They have the brightest minds. Many of these young men and women understand profit. They understand having profit is a benefit and advantage. It is an access to income. Making money on something that will turn a profit, they understand the benefits to making money. They understand the basic principles. They understand the language of revenue concept, and they understand that, in order to make profit, you can't do it by yourself. It takes teamwork and strategy. Working in Corporate America is about making the gain. It's about dealing with the competitors. Whenever you have a business that's bringing in profit, you also have someone else who wants to get a piece of the action. That's competition because they want to be better than you are. That's why you have to stay a step ahead of the competition because it's fierce.

Young people can identify with these concepts. They have to stay a step ahead of the game. If you take some of these young people with their brilliant minds, one such example is hip-hop mogul Russell Simmons, CEO of Def Jam, which took in over $200 million in 1998.And the count is rising. He said in an interview that the creative people who are great are talking about the youth culture in a way that makes sense, and that happens to be the rappers. All rappers are not negative. Some are just trying to open up our understanding to their negative environment, abuse, drugs, alcohol, and police brutality, that is, things some of us will never experience in a lifetime. These young people see it every day, and this is their way of expressing what they see and feel in lyrics. Some have brilliant minds.

Consider the numbers. In 1998, for the first time ever, rap outsold what previously had been America's top-selling format, country music. Rap sold more than a million CDs, tapes, and albums, compared with 72 million for country. Rap sales increased a stunning 31 percent from 1997 to 1998, in contrast to 2 percent gains for country, 6 percent for rock, and 9 percent for the music industry overall. Rapper Jay-Z, whose album, *Vol. 2 ... Hard Knock Life* (Def Jam) has sold more than 3 million copies, boasts, "There is a difference when it comes to hip-hop. Rap is a form of rhythmic speaking in rhyme; hip-hop refers to the backing music for rap, which is often composed of a collage of excerpts, or 'samples, 'from other songs. Hip-hop also refers to the culture of rap. The two terms are similar but not completely interchangeable. Hip-hop represents a realignment of America's cultural aesthetics. Rap songs deliver the message repeatedly to keep it real."One such young man stated in an interview, "I'm not a role model," rapper-mogul-aspiring NBA player Master P says. "But I see myself as a resource for kids. They can say, 'Master P has been through a lot, but he changed his life. And look at him now. I can do the same thing.' I think anyone who's a success is an inspiration."

I also admire Mary J. Blige. She has been the queen of hip-hop for decades. Mary is using her voice to empower a generation of women. She is truly a bridge builder of hope. For the young women rising in today's generation, she is a witness that God can bring you from a world filled with oppression, worry, and stress to a world filled with love and happiness. She lets us know in her lyrics that problems will be there, but you have the power to overcome any obstacle that tries to keep you enslaved. Mary is truly beautiful.

In order to understand what these young men and women are trying to communicate, we need to stop being critical of all of them and sit back and listen to the lyrics. In order to understand rap, you have to go back to its roots in the late 1970s, a time of change and transformation. It was the end of Jim Crow and the beginning of change. In 1979, the first two rap records appeared, *King Tim III (Personality Jock)* recorded by the Fatback Band and *Rapper's Delight* by the Sugarhill Gang. The message was in the music. If you listen to James Brown, Marvin Gaye, Curtis Mayfield, and the O'Jays, to name a few among the greats, their messages of the time was in the music, just as it is in this generation. Their message was about love and awareness. Some rap artists are trying to bring positive change to their generation; others have sold out for profit.

Before we become judge and jury, we need to listen to what the young people are trying to say. I was very critical when it came to rap music. I didn't want my children playing such garbage. I didn't want it in my house. I forbade them to buy it, but years later, when my children were grown and gone, I just sat down one day and listened to this song on the radio. It was garbage to me, but the things they were singing about, they had to live in this garbage everyday, and they were trying to give us a picture of the environment most of these young men and women came from. Not only did they come out and succeed, but they are reaching out to generations of young people, encouraging them to succeed and be successful.

I say, "More power to you."

I began to understand what they were singing about. It was their message to the world. Knowledge that I had been ignorant to, but now I understood. I do not agree when it comes to men addressing women as "bitches" and "hoes," using the word "niggas," and calling your friends "dogs."As I stated earlier, not every artist in the rap field are calling women bitches, hoes, and niggas. I understand your language of communication, but we as a generation of people have come too far to be addressed in such a way. Your past generation knows what it is like to be addressed in such a way. You have only heard of the stories, but you were not there in the times. There have been many blood, sweat, and tears behind calling a person a nigger. The definition of the word "nigger" is a highly offensive term for a black person and anyone who is dark skinned. And for you to use it so freely, it's ashame, especially if it's being addressed to your own race.

I do understand that there are still injustices today, but what you say and do will make a difference in your generation and the next to come. It's all about change, changing for a positive. You are brilliant young men and women who deserve a chance at opportunity. It will not knock on your door. You have to grab it when it comes. These young men and women could be successful entrepreneurs, turning their negative into positive and equipping them with the knowledge they need to succeed in marketing principles. They have the minds to be great. Just as Mr. Russell Simmons, Jay-Z, and all the other successful entrepreneurs became, there are so many fields to choose from. All you have to do is come up with an idea, one that makes money. God has implanted a measure of potential within all of his children, and everybody is his children, no matter what the color.

So many times, we, as adults, just give up and throw up our hands. Some even come to the point of washing their hands of their children. How sad. Someone had to be patient and love you through your craziness. It's amazing how we are so soon to forget our past. Never give up hope when it comes to your children. Never stop loving them. They need you in the midst of their change. If these young men and women cannot find the love, attention, and support at home, then they will be introduced to the impurities of the streets, or sheep in wolf's clothing.

Parents, don't wait until your home get out of control. Don't wait until you lose your children to ask yourself what went wrong. Don't let it be too late when all you had to do was take the time and give your children your attention. Learn to listen sometimes instead of fussing and cussing. Listen to your child. It does not mean that things will always go their way because children must follow certain rules. It is the governing principle. There are rules to any game. There are rules that have to be followed in the home as well. There have to be rules, or else chaos will follow. Our children should not be afraid to express their feeling for fear of being rejected, ostracized, or criticized. Allow your children to able to come to you in the crisis of their lives. Love them enough to see them through their problems.

Parents, learn to take the control back in your homes. You can't be your child's best friend. You're a parent. You are supposed to be what keeps the fibers together. Be aware of what your children are getting involved in. Don't be so busy that you ignore your children. You want to know where your children are going and the type of people they are involving themselves in. Teach your children about being accountable for their actions and being responsible for carrying out home chores. If you don't teach them about being responsible, they will become lazy. How can they possibly learn anything when you're always doing things for them?

We had four children, and when they were at home, they had chores. I had a list and expected each and every one of them to complete their chores. They had to keep their rooms clean, and they took turns taking out the garbage. I had four children, and there were enough chores to go around. There was no leisure time until they completed their homework and chores. Then they were allowed to go have recreation time. I would rotate their duties so each one would have a different chore each week. Some children never grow up with a sense of responsibility because their parents do everything for them. Mothers clean the house, take out the garbage, and clean the whole house while the children are sitting down watching cartoons.

I was always in my children's business. I wanted to know everything they brought in the house. They cleaned their room, but when they left for school, I conducted a thorough search of their rooms. I was worse than a dog sniffing for drugs. Most of the time, they thought they were sneaking around behind my back, but I busted them every time. Inspector Burley was on her job. I knew what was coming into my house, and if they hid anything, they did it very well. When they left for school, I would find whatever was not supposed to be in their room.

You have some children do everything under the sun, smuggling in weapons and drugs, sneaking in and out of the house, and having sex in the next room while the parents are asleep. They don't have a clue … until they get a knock at the door with the police informing them regarding their children's activities. Parents, it's time to get involved with your children's lives.

PERSONALITY DIFFERENCES

As our children begin to grow and mature, their personality will change as well. As parents, we have to learn how to give our children freedom to express their feelings, their likes and dislikes, what they want to be, and the things they hope to accomplish in the future. They need space to express how they feel about themselves and others around them.

When our children were growing up, we had family time together once a week. During this time, the children were allowed to express their feelings. They were free to discuss any issues without fearing they would get scolded. Family time was open season. They expressed their feelings concerning school, classmates, and teachers. They expressed things that were going on at home, from weekly chores, which they thought was totally unfair; their feelings of how Mom and Dad could make their lives a little more pleasant; boyfriends and girlfriends; and sex. You name it, they had questions. My husband and I prayed to God to give us the right answers for every question they asked.

Family time really gave my husband and me a chance to understand how the children really felt about certain issues. It also caused us to recognize the gap in communication between our children and ourselves. We began to understand through our children that they had needs as well, and we had to allow them to express how they felt. One of my daughters had anger and resentment built up inside of her for years. She never forgot an incident that occurred many years before.

In previous chapters, we discussed planting positive or negative seeds. I planted one of those seeds without realizing what I had done. Mothers, you know how it is when you're tired from doing household chores all day, cooking, cleaning, changing diapers, and washing. It seems like a day's work never get done. Well, it was one of those days. I was being pulled in different directions, and everyone needed my attention. I just wanted a moment to myself. In the midst of my frustration, I said something out of anger, which I didn't mean at all. I forgot the incident, but my daughter never forgot what was said.

After a number of years, my daughter brought me into remembrance of what I had said to her. It broke me to pieces because I didn't realize she had held onto this pain for so long. What I felt was harmless, she took to mind. Sometimes we can say things without thinking, such damaging things like, "I wish you were like Missy Sue ... You're going to grow up to be just like you're no-good father." These types of words can be damaging to our children. You will go on and forget, just as I did, but the damage has already been stored in their little minds.

I apologized over and over. I hugged and kissed her and let her know how much I loved her. I expressed to her how I never meant to hurt her. My daughter forgave me, but I never forgot the expression and hurt on her face. I started to listen to my children, and in the moment of anger, I would be careful of the things I would say. When I was wrong, I would sit down with my children and explain to them that parents makes mistakes as well. We were not all perfect, and I would ask them to forgive me. I was never too proud to say I was wrong and ask for forgiveness. Sometimes we, as parents, can put ourselves on a big pedestal with our children and others around us. We pretend we are perfect and can do nothing wrong. We never make mistakes, and we go through life with our children, never owning up to our responsibilities. We become set in our ways, and we wonder why our children will not come to us in time of trouble. Just being honest and admitting we are not perfect when it comes to parenting and being honest with our children will cover a multitude of problems. With each experience comes lessons to be learned, with time comes experience, and with experience comes patience.

Pretty soon, our children began to open up and communicate with us. We learned a lot about our children and ourselves. We learned we could not engage ourselves with other things and neglect our children's needs, taking them for granted and just assuming they were happy.

We went to church religiously. We were affiliated with the Church of God in Christ. When the church doors opened, we were there. As I stated before, my husband was a local minister in our church, helping his father, our pastor at the time. My husband and I were on various boards of the church. My hands were equally full, assisting my mother-in-law with various projects. The church was small. Everything that needed to be done, we were asked to do it. We dragged our children everywhere we went. They did their homework in church, and the church was their second home because we were there so regularly. Their beds were the church pew. I always bought a blanket or two. At times, our children resented us for going to church so regularly. We attended church four days out of the week. That didn't include district meetings, choir rehearsals, and revivals.

At times, we exhausted our own selves. Our children made a pledge among them that, when they got grown, they would never attend a Pentecostal church again, certainly not like the church we were members of. They felt they had no freedom because they were restricted from doing certain things .Our organization was known as the no-can-do church. They had strict rules they observed and practiced daily. In those days, women were not allowed to wear pants and makeup. Going to the picture show was a sin. If we put other activities before the church, we were going to hell. Playing cards, dominoes, or Monopoly was a sin. If you listened to any other type of music other than church music, they felt it was the devil's music, and you were going straight to hell. If they heard you were doing anything else other than what the church taught, you were on the altar until they felt like God had purged away your sins.

Thank God that the church has changed over the years .It's not as strict as it once was, and they figured out that salvation is not in what you wear and how you look. Salvation comes from the heart. We're saved by grace.

These were some of the conditions our children were subject to, and they resented it. We didn't have any family time together. Communication became unbearable because, at some point, we were forcing our children to go where they did not feel included. The church had functions for the children, but to them, it was boring. Looking back now, I agree with them. My husband saw the effect it was having on the children, so we started cutting back on some of our activities in order to spend more time with them. The moment we started giving our children our attention, we could instantly see changes. We would help them with their homework. Except there were things I did not understand. Dad had to step in to help. They helped each other with their homework. We shared in some of their school activities. We began to share interest in their friends and their first jobs. We began to feel like a family again. Things were not perfect, but it was a start. They all graduated and received their diplomas. Our daughters enlisted in the United States Air Force; our son enlisted in the United States Army shortly after graduating from high school.

To parents committed to certain religious institutions, don't lose your children in the church. Don't be so caught up in the emotion and forget the needs of your children. It's good to shout and dance, but when the jubilation is over, the real world is still present. Our problems are still there to face. It's not all in the emotion, but it's learning to walk with God, having the kind of faith that, whatever you are going through, he is able to deliver according to his will. In the meantime, you have to live life in the real world until God does what he's going to do concerning your situation. Don't enjoy the fruits of the spirit shouting and dancing while your own children, your seed, sits idle and empty in the church pew. Share your children's dreams, ideas, and passions. Let them know that God loves them, too .Our children are our future. They are the leaders of tomorrow, and we cannot ignore them.

Give your children a chance to express themselves. Allow them to un-bottle the anger stored up on the inside of them. We wonder how children can be so angry that they go on shooting sprees in the schools. We wonder how children can be so depressed. They have thoughts of committing suicide. Could it be that the parents are too busy to listen? What happens when they get out of control and explode? Could these tragedies been prevented if the parents had been doing their part?

Parents, I beseech you, by the mercies of God, don't give up on your children so easily and throw up your hands. I see so many parents get frustrated when their children are out of control. They are ready to throw in the towel and ship the child off to boot camp for troubled children, alternative schools, or anything to get rid of the problem. They feel like they have wasted their lives on this troubled child. They want someone else to take on the responsibility of solving their problems.

You need God's wisdom and directions concerning your child. Your child needs your unconditional love and support through their storms in life. In the midst of every storm, prayer will get you through. God can calm any storm. It's not always about you, yourself, and you. It's about fighting for the survival of your children. You have a major task ahead of you. Don't be so quick to throw in the towel. The devil is out to destroy your children's destiny. He will try to steal, kill, and destroy what God has ordained, but you have the power to keep your children covered through the power of prayer. Our children are gifts from God. Don't lose them to the devil because you're placing your needs ahead of them. They will later appreciate you for taking interest, setting aside quality time to spend with them, and allowing them to express their selves. Your sacrifices and prayers will pay off one day.

Parenting is not an easy job because you are making decisions in your children's best interest, ones they may not always agree with. You are molding them into adulthood. You are preparing them for the future. There are only two ways you can prepare them; you can prepare them to succeed or to fail. So many times, we try to build relationships with our children based on friendship. We want them to feel free to come to us and talk to us about anything, but there is a border of separation between being a parent and being a child. You're not their friend, buddy, or partner. You're their parent, and you are responsible for teaching and equipping them with the needed skills, qualities, and responsibilities that involves being a parent caring for the needs of your child. Some parents give their children too much liberty. From ages sixteen and younger, they come and go as they please. They bring home whoever they want whenever they want. Some parents even allow boyfriends and girlfriends to move into the home. Some parents even party, drink, and smoke a little weed with their children. It is a sad situation to see, but you see it all the time. The talk shows have really uncovered the dysfunctional family. Children have totally lost respect for their parents, but when problems come their way, the first place they will point the finger to is their parents.

"If you had been there for me and acted like my mother or father instead of my friend, I would not be the way I am. If you had been more strict ..."They would lay it on you, so why be angry when they are only telling the truth?

Parents need to step up to the plate and be the parents, and if you don't know what it is to be a parent, a number of resources can assist you in learning. In each generation, children are different. You can't raise your children the way your parents raised you. I tried to raise my children the way my mother raised me, and if I had it all to do again, I would do some things differently. The way my mother raised me, she would be serving time in prison. By today's standards, it's labeled as child abuse, and I was whipped, not spanked. A spanking is when you are slapped on the buttocks; a whipping is when you're being beat with belts, extension cards, and tree branches, whatever they could find to beat your butt. I would sit and count all my whelps on my legs and arms. Back in the day, it was normal, especially in black family homes. It was not labeled child abuse, and you had better not suggest to your parents you were being abused, or they would really abuse you. Today, we cannot raise children the way we were raised. I believe in discipline, but I believe there is a proper way to discipline a child.

Some will state that you can't raise a black child the same way a white child is raised. I totally disagree. One day at the store, I cringed when I saw a little six-year-old disrespecting his mother, falling out in the store. Having a fit bothers me. If my children had did that to me when they were small, wherever they acted a fool, I was going to act one, too. I kept my belt in my purse just in case. They knew their mother loved them, but I was not going to stand for any nonsense. Thinking back, I know I would have done things differently. A timeout may not have worked, but taking away something they liked would have certainly gotten their attention.

Never discipline your child when you're angry. My mother used to whip me until she got tired. She was blowing for breath. The louder I screamed, the harder she whipped. It was a mental thing with me. I figured the louder I screamed, she would eventually stop. It never worked. She tore my behind up.

I would be screaming over and over and over, "I'm sorry, Mama. I won't do it no more."

I was a hardheaded little girl, and I knew that, when she got through with me, I would find something else to get in trouble for. I knew I was going to get in trouble. I also liked playing ball with my friends. My mother wanted me home by six for dinner, which was too early to come home.

I knew I was in trouble when I could hear Mama calling me from way up the street, "Linda Kay, you better get your behind home now."

I just bid my friends bye and told them I would see them the next day because I knew Mama was going to whip my behind. So when I had children of my own, I became the spitting image of my mother, a no-nonsense parent, but today, many resources can help us be better parents to our children. Resources can help us communicate effectively with our children. There are support groups so women can share how they can be effective mothers in their parenting skills. The children of today are much wiser than when we were growing up.

Parents, your hard work will pay off as long as you ask God to order your steps. Ask God's directions in how to properly raise your children. God always has a master plan. He will manifest his plan and purpose for your family. God is about building and strengthening the family unit. Don't try to win over your children's affections by getting on their level. Don't try to be anything else but a loving parent to them, and when you have given all you know to give your love and support, you have given them your best. You have set the foundation for their future.

IN THE IMAGE OF YOU

Our children are our future. They are our hope for tomorrow. They are the image of you. Whatsoever you produce inside of them, it will bring forth fruit knowing that the labor of your love will pay off abundantly. Parenting is not an easy job. I haven't begun to tell you the whole story. You can buy books and books on parenting. It's only when you begin the journey and experience it for yourself that you will begin to understand what parenting is all about. You will make mistakes over and over again, but never be too proud to let your children know you're not perfect. Let them see through you what true forgiveness is all about. It all starts with you. Love will cover a multitude of mistakes, and most of all, making God the center of your home will make the difference. When you are building on a firm foundation, you can't go wrong. There will be times you will laugh, cry, or try to solve every problem. Your presence can be influential, effective, and persuasive. Your children will look back and appreciate those times you spent with them. It will bring tears to your eyes when you see them make major accomplishments, watch them walk on stage to receive their diplomas, pursue their own careers, and form their own families.

Having you there guiding them into their destiny will be all worth the wait, and with each child, there will be a different story to tell. With each child, you will learn from past mistakes. They will be your joy, life, and love, and no matter how different they all are, they are all yours. Sometimes you will wish you could send them back to the sender, but the sender gives them to you as a seed to cultivate that they may one day produce good fruit. They are gifts from the Father, and he has made you a watchman to keep watch over his best interest. God has entrusted you to take care of his seeds.

Our children are gifts from God, so don't give up on your children just because they're not meeting your expectations. You don't know what these young men and women will become. Keep positive words flowing into their spirits, and bring out the best in them. The things you speak have the power to heal or kill their spirits. Never give up on your children because you never know what tomorrow will bring. Whatever you instill into your children, they will become the product of what you produce. You never graduate from parenting. It's a continued education even after the last child has gone. Your job goes on and on. You will soon become an extension of your children's children, distributing your knowledge and wisdom to the next generation.

There will always be new things to learn when it comes to parenting. It is a lifelong learning process. Give your children your quality time. Never allow other people, places, or things to get in the way of the relationship you have with your children. Let your children know you care and you will be there in the good times and bad. You will be there to console them when disappointments come their way. You will dry their tears just by the words you speak. Just having you there makes the difference. Be there to encourage them though their journeys in life. Each one of us has a different journey in life, and your children will experience theirs. Life is a process of passing from one level to another, from innocence to mature awareness.

When the last child spreads his or her wings and flies from the nest, the joy you shared will become a sweet memory. Cherish the time you have. No matter what life may bring their way, your love and protection will carry them through their journey. The things you instill into your children today will carry them the rest of the way. It will carry them into their divine destiny, making a difference in the lives of others for generations to come, but it all has to start with you. When you know where you're going, you can cause that same spirit to flow freely into your children's spirit, instilling the keys to success into their spirits.

PART FOUR

IN THE SEASONS
OF YOUR LIFE

M any people feel like the world stops rotating once the children grow up and leave home. You have spent a majority of your life raising a family. Your very being was centered on meeting your children's needs. You nurtured them when they were infants, you changed diapers, you washed and fed them, you dressed them in their little outfits, you rocked them to sleep, you read bedtime stories to them, you stayed up in the middle of the night when they were congested with colds and fever, and your prayers got them through the night. You were there on their first day of school, you had your hands full baking cookies for the PTA and helping with homework, and you were the carpool mom dropping them off at different school activities. You first told your child about the birds and the bees, and you first explained to your daughters that they were not going to bleed to death when they experienced their first menstrual cycle. You stood as a mother hen when they brought home their first date. You were there for the high school proms, making sure everything went right. You shared in their excitement when they got their first jobs. You were there as they walked the stage to receive their high school diplomas. Then you were there as they walked down the aisle on their wedding day, vowing to love and cherish someone else until death do them part. You took care and protected their every needs. You watched them grow and develop. You knew the day would come when you would finally cut the umbilical cord of your children's lives.

Now your babies have grown up to be young, mature adults. You were there when the first grandchild introduced himself or herself to the world. God blessed you to see many more grandchildren.

You have been a major part of your children's lives, and now they are all grown and gone. And now you feel all alone. You feel like you're not needed as much anymore. You feel as if life has passed you by. You have given your life to helping the family, and now they're all grown and gone. You have given a lifetime of yourself, but life does not stop when the children leave home. As one chapter closes, another one opens, and you will continue to make the difference in the lives of your family and others around you. It's your time to kick back and relax. It's time for you to do things for your pleasure. The physical and emotional pressure you have placed on yourself, devoting your life to the well-being of your children, you have placed yourself last. In order to meet your children's needs, you have sacrificed yourself. You have strived, and you have accomplished the things you have set out to do, being a good parent to your children. You have been there to wipe the tears from their eyes when things were not going quite their way. You were there pushing and encouraging them. You had faith in whatever good things they did. You had a plan for their lives, and that plan was for them to be successful. You were fussy and overprotective when it came to the people they associated their lives with. Sometimes you were your children's worst nightmare, but they didn't see what you already knew. You were partial as to who they dated and married because you had a plan. Nothing or no one could interfere with your plans for your children's lives. It was your prayers that they succeed in life to be fruitful in whatsoever things they touched. So far you have accomplished what you have set out to do, to make productive young adults out of your children. You have equipped them to go on to the next level of their lives to pursue their dreams and be young achievers. You have taught them that they can do anything with God as their commander-in-chief.

Now it's time for them to leave the nest and learn to fly on their own. Our children are young eagles, and we must give them space to let them soar. We must step back to see what lessons they have learned. Are they prepared from the years of learning? Did they pay attention, or did they ignore the facts? Now is the testing time, and now it is your job to step back and allow them to show you what they have learned.

It's your season now to fulfill your dreams and desires. Now you can do the things you placed on a back burner in order to raise a family. Perhaps you had a desire to pursue a degree in education. You thought about going back to college. What about those dreams you had of one day starting your own business? Remember when you said you were going back to the work field when the children are all grown and gone? Whatever your desires were, it is never too late to start again. I remember sitting around the house feeling sorry for myself. I sat depressed around the house for weeks. I didn't know what to do with myself. I had enough things to do to keep me busy. I had a full-time job working with a successful corporate company. I now had time to catch up on my writing and finally do some things for myself, but I still had a deep void when the last child left.

When she left for military training, I felt I was not needed any longer. For twenty-four hours a day, seven days a week, three hundred and sixty-five days of the year, my whole life was centered around my family and meeting their needs. Instead of preparing dinner for six, now I was preparing dinner for just my husband and me. It took me some time of not getting into the habit of preparing large meals. Even after the children had left home, I would still find myself preparing large meal. As a result, we would have a refrigerator full of leftovers.

At the time, my husband was thrilled we had an empty nest, and he thought of a million things we could do with our time together. For him, it was like winning the lotto. He couldn't wait to get started. The children were always at home. There was never a quiet moment, but when they all left home, it seemed like the atmosphere was so gloomy. They were in the military, and their duties scattered them all around the state. During my lonely times, I would pick up the phone, call them, and tell them how much I missed them. I had not heard from them. They would always laugh and say, "Mother, you just called the day before yesterday." I would always wonder what they were doing and what their day was like. When I was at work, I would wonder what they were doing in the middle of the night. It took a period of about twelve months.

Then I began to come out of my shell and realize they were gone but not far. I could always pick up the phone, night or day. I had to realize they were not babies, but now they were young adults with their own lives and their own families. So I decided to get up and do something with myself. I shook off that depression, realized I was not finished living, fixed myself up, and began to make plans for the future. It was so much that my hand could find for me to do. I definitely was not ready for a rocking chair. I had my writing to catch up with, some books to be published. I had my sewing, some designs to be created, and I had so much to do.

My children are always with me. Their spirits are with me. Even when they forget to call home, I know they are just fine because we raised them well.

Life does not stop when the children leave home. You have so much more to give. You have much of your spirit to pass on to others. You have so much knowledge and wisdom to impart and invest to other young men and women, sons and daughters. You hold a wealth of information. Raising your family has qualified you to give advice and communicate the positives and negatives. You have become an educator of life learning, and you can share your ideas to another generation, your grandchildren, those who come into your life. Life does not stop when the children leave home. It all gets better with time. It's about growing old gracefully. God has blessed you to raise your family, and now he has blessed you to enjoy the benefits of your labor. These are the golden years. You only have one life to live. Live it to the fullest. Take advantage of opportunities as they come. These are some of the keys to triumphant family living. As long as God is at the center of your life, he will direct your path, and God's good pleasure ushers you into your divine destiny.

I pray that this book has been a blessing to you. It was my pleasure sharing my personal experiences with you, and I pray this book will be a guide to help you in the future. Always remember that God is the commander-in-chief of your life. It is his good pleasure that you be successful and achieve those God-given abilities, so allow him to guide you to the next level of your life. God has given you the potential to reach your destiny. You have been chosen to succeed.